EIRINI PRESS

Patriotism for Grownups: How to be a Citizen in the 21ˢᵗ Century (with Eda LeShan), Trafford, 2005.

The Pattern of Evil: Myth, Social Perception and the Holocaust, XLibris, 2005.

A New Science of the Paranormal: The Promise of Psychical Research, Quest Books, 2009.

The Majorica Conference on the Implications of PSI, (Co-edited with Arthur Twitchell), iWrite Publications, 2012.

LANDSCAPES
of the MIND

The Faces of Reality

Eirini Press (Eirinipress.com)
510 Long Hill Rd.
Guilford, CT 06437

Cover design: Tarol Samuelson

Library of Congress Control Number: 2012938801

Landscapes of the Mind/Lawrence LeShan

ISBN 978-0-9799989-8-0
    1. LeShan, Lawrence
    2. Psychology: Consciousness
    3. Perception
    4. Philosophy: Metaphysics

LANDSCAPES
of the MIND

The Faces of Reality

by Lawrence LeShan

EIRINI PRESS

To
Giambattista Vico
(1668-1744)
who first articulated the concepts
that led to this book.

The central puzzle is not about 'how consciousness evolved,' nor is it about 'how would we know it was there if we didn't happen to be aware of it already,' though both of those questions have raised a lot of dust. The central worry is: 'How can we rationally speak of our inner experience at all? How can we regard our inner world — the world of our everyday experience — as somehow forming part of the larger, public world which is now described in terms that seem to leave no room for it? On what map can both these areas be shown and intelligibly related?'

— Mary Midgley

The purpose of this book is to attempt to respond to these questions.

Contents

Acknowledgements

In a work like this it is impossible to fully give credit where credit is due. Many people have studied, from one viewpoint or another, the area I am here attempting to explore. Some of these I have experienced directly through their publications and these I have tried to at least mention. Others I have experienced only through their effect on people whose work I have read. Often I do not even know their names in spite of the fact that I have benefited from their work.

The sharp intellectual eye and unwavering support of Ada Nicolescu has been of critical value in the development of this book.

I also owe much thanks to Mary Midgley, David Pruett, Jonathan Bricklin, Stanley Kripper, and Ruth Bollatino for their helpful comments and critiques.

One person I particularly wish to thank is Eda Le-Shan. For years she listened to, and commented on, my confused descriptions of what I was trying to do in coming to grips with the issues of this book. She steadily over these years encouraged me to stay with the exploration and to keep trying to develop it.

From the physicist-philosopher Henry Margenau I learned very much, both specifically and generally. I benefited greatly from his friendship and from the example of his dedication to the best in science and philosophy. To have worked with this good man whose mind was like a soaring eagle was one of the great experiences of my life.

I am grateful for the extraordinary editorial abilities

that Denise Meyer brought to this book. And without the technical skills and extraordinary patience of Susan Gordis the work would have been stillborn.

I.
You and Your World Pictures:
How Things Are and Work

Whoever aspires to understand man...must throw
overboard all immobile concepts
and learn to think in ever-shifting terms.
— *Ortega y Gasset*

John Psmith, consulting engineer, has come home after
a day's work at his office. He is sitting in his living room,
idly leafing through the day's paper, and relaxing. There
is a cloud on the horizon of his mind. He has heard on
the local news several times in the last few days that there
have been a number of cases of meningitis in the neigh-
borhood. He is worried about his four-year-old daughter who is upstairs. Should he, he wonders, have kept
her home from nursery school until there was no more
threat of an epidemic?

As he thinks about this, he hears the sound of the
child crying. He gets up and begins to go up the stairs.
He is suddenly terribly frightened. He mutters to himself, "Please, I'll do anything, but don't let Amy have

meningitis. If it has to be, let it be me instead of her. She's too small."

It is plain that Psmith is praying. He is pleading with something outside of himself and even offering a bargain. We all understand what is happening. We might well do the same thing under similar circumstances.

Psmith is, at this moment, deeply sincere. He feels, thinks and acts as if he knows that there is something or someone to pray to and that results can be obtained by prayer. Where this entity is located is not a real question or a matter of any interest to Psmith. *Distance*, how far away this entity is, whether it be measured in inches or in light years, is not a factor in his perceptions. As a matter of fact, *numbers* simply do not apply to anything during the moments when it makes sense to Psmith to pray. The idea of measuring or numbering anything is simply not relevant.

This is a far cry from how Psmith perceived the world and reacted to it during his day at the office. The two world pictures are very different. As he sat at his desk he did not believe that wishes or prayer could change anything. He might wish deeply that the steel rods he is planning to use in the machine he is designing were stronger, but he is clear that no wish or prayer will make them so. There is simply nothing or no one "out there" to take note of his wishes, no matter how strong they are, and change the strength of the rods. If he wants stronger rods he will have to substitute another metal or another thickness. And he knows exactly how to do this.

Further, everything can be, and is best done, in numbers. He knows the numerical relationship between the thickness of the rods and their breaking points, the number of rods he will need, the number of days it will take the factory to make them, the number of miles away the factory is and what this means in days from manufacture to delivery. In short he is in a world where everything of importance can be numbered and expressed in exact quantitative terms. These two views of how-the-world-is-and-works, these two world pictures, are clearly very different.

Psmith arrives upstairs and finds to his great relief that the child is not sick. She has awakened in the night confused and frightened. He takes her in his arms and says, "It's all right. Everything is all right."

Psmith is now perceiving and reacting to the world in a third way. In deep sincerity, as he holds Amy to his chest and cuddles her, in both body language and words he is saying that they both live in a friendly universe in which love protects against all problems and that all is well and will be well. This is the truth as he knows it at this moment. It is very different from the way he knows the world as he works at his desk. In that world picture they will both eventually die and be annihilated and eventually they and their culture and even their planet will be forgotten dust. You cannot know that and also feel that the universe is friendly and that love solves all problems.

A second difference between the world as he knows

it at his desk and as he knows it while reassuring Amy is that in the reassurance world, numbers and measurement are again irrelevant. Counting is not a part of reality.

Before he returns downstairs, he reads Amy her favorite fairy tale. Even knowing the ending, they become anxiously involved in the Prince's quest for the owner of the slipper. (Just as two adults, knowing the ending, may become deeply involved in Othello's doubts and jealousy. Every time I see a performance of *La Bohème* I find myself hoping that Mimi will recover and that she and Rodolfo will continue to live together.)

So far we have seen Psmith construe and react to the world in three different ways. In spite of their differences Psmith, when he was using each one, knew he was correctly perceiving reality and that the picture of the construction of reality he was using at that moment was the only true and valid one.

Later that evening, Psmith and his wife go out dancing. Most of the evening he dances fairly well, enjoys himself, talks with his wife and lets his thoughts wander over many areas. At one moment, however, he realizes that for some time previously things have been very different. He was fully alert and awake, but thinking of nothing. He was dancing from his toes to his scalp. He was totally and fully involved in only one thing and that was the dancing. During that period, he danced far better than he usually did, and he and his wife responded to each other as if there had been some kind of instantaneous telepathy between them. He had no idea what brought this change on, only a very vague idea of how long it went on, and after it was over, he felt charged up, generally very good and a little bit tired. If we analyze what the world was like for Psmith during this time, we find that he and the music and his wife and the floor and the other dancers were one entity and there were no sharp lines between them, no clear beginnings and ends. There could be no counting because there were no separate entities to count. Everything flowed into everything else, and the universe was a seamless garment. There was no such thing as willing, as "executive decision making," because this would have meant a separation, a "doer" and a "done unto" and these did not exist. Will was not a factor in this world construction.

Late that night, after going to sleep, Psmith has a dream. In the dream he is walking along a beach and a mermaid, beautiful and erotic, comes out of the ocean and sings to him. Then a car comes down the beach driven by his long-dead older brother and then they are in an airplane and the stewardess is a tall kangaroo.

Everything in this dream is as real as everything else. The mermaid and the car are equally real. In fact, once anything is clearly conceived of, it immediately attains full reality status. At his work at his desk for something to be real it had to have consistent effects on other things. At his desk a desert mirage would not have been real because it did not have consistent effects. The definition of "real" differs in the different world pictures.

Measurement is also quite different in the world picture of the dream and the world picture used by the engineer while working at his desk. It is generally not possible in the dream to find out how far apart two things are in space or in time. Are the airplane and the car a mile apart or more or less? In how many minutes does one follow the other? We cannot tell. And the numbers of things also are different in the two world pictures. In the dreamworld there may be three or four of something, but after that there seems to be only "many" or "a great many." Distances and times may be "long" or "short," but not twenty-seven inches or forty-three and a half miles or seventeen hours and four minutes.

We shall return to Psmith and his strange but familiar life from time to time in this book, but in order to begin to understand what is going on here and its implications, let us approach the matter from another angle. Let us look at how the majority of the citizens of a whole country may sometimes change the world they perceive and react to in an apparently synchronized manner. We will take the example of how, in the waking state, the world is generally defined in Europe and America during peacetime and when we are in a war in which we are emotionally involved. Rather than describing the world pictures such as we used in the day of John Psmith, for this examination I shall proceed differently. I will examine some of the characteristics of a generally agreed upon concept of how-reality-is-and-works and compare them to the pictures used in peacetime and in wartime.

In Peacetime

1. Good and Evil have many shades of grey. Many opinions and groups with different ideas are legitimate. Things and opinions are seen as relatively good and bad, satisfactory or unsatisfactory, stupid or intelligent.

2. "Now" is pretty much like other times. There are more of some things, less of others, but the differences are quantitative.

3. The great forces of nature, such as God or human evolution, are not particularly involved in our disputes.

In Wartime

Good and Evil are "We" and "They." There are no innocent bystanders; you are for us or against us. The crucial parts of the world are divided into black and white. Opinions on this are absolutely right or wrong.

"Now" is special, qualitatively different from all other times. Everything is cast in the balance; who wins now wins forever. It is the time of the final battle between good and evil, of Armageddon, of Ragnarok, of the War to End Wars. "It is the final battle," says the Internationale.

"God Wills It," *"Dieu et mon droit,"* "History fights on our side," "Manifest Destiny," and other such slogans indicate our belief that the great forces of the cosmos are for "U"s and against "Them."

In Peacetime	*In Wartime*
4. When this present period is over, things will go on pretty much as they have in the past.	When this war is over, everything will be vastly different. If we win, much better; if we lose, terribly worse. The world will be deeply changed by what we do here. Winning or losing will change the meaning of the past and the shape of the future.
5. There are many problems to be solved and their relative importance varies from day to day. Life is essentially complex with many foci.	There is only one major problem to be solved. All others are secondary. Life is essentially simple. It has one major focus.
6. All people act from pretty much the same motives.	"They" act from a wish for power. "We" act from self-defense, benevolence, and reasons of common decency and morality.
7. Problems start on many levels, e.g., economic, political, personal, and must be dealt with on these levels.	The real problem started with an act of will on the part of the enemy and can only be solved by breaking his will or by making him helpless to act on it.

In Peacetime	*In Wartime*
8. We are concerned with the causes of problems we are trying to solve.	We are not concerned with causes, only with outcomes.
9. We can talk with those with whom we disagree. Negotiation is possible.	Since the enemy is evil, he naturally lies. Communication is not possible.
10. All people are fundamentally the same. Differences are quantitative.	"We" and "They" are qualitatively different, so different that the same actions are "good" when we do them, "evil" when the enemy does them. There is doubt that they and we really belong to the same species.

What I have been describing here is clearly a shift in our world picture, our perception of reality. It is essentially a change from structuring the world in the way we generally do in our waking state to the basic structure we see in fairy tale and myth. The way-things-are, the rules for living, the morality which guides us, are very different in these two situations. The difference is much greater than one would assume from the bare descriptions of some of its facets which I have listed in the previous pages. Sweet and adorable Dorothy, who we all love, and who none of us criticizes or condemns, travels from one organization of reality in Kansas to another in Oz. While there she kills two people, the Wicked Witches of the East and West and takes from their bodies what she wants. From the first she steals shoes, from the second a broomstick. Since they are not only bad, but in a world picture where "bad" means "ultimately and completely evil," we applaud. But there was also a bad person in Kansas (Miss Gulch), who tried to have Toto killed, and who bedeviled Dorothy quite severely. What would have happened to our feelings if Dorothy had killed her, even accidentally, in Kansas and then robbed her body? At the least, most of us would have wavered in our unqualified approval. Similarly in wartime. The enemy is so completely, so mythically evil that anything we do to him is not only justified, but good. Rollo May put it:

> At the outset of every war . . . we hastily transform our enemy into the image of the daimonic; and then, since it is the devil we are fighting, we can shift onto a war footing without asking ourselves all the troublesome and spiritual questions that the war arouses. We no longer have to face the realization that those we are killing are persons like ourselves.[1]

This statement is true, but leaves out an essential fact. The "daimonic" can only fit into a certain view of reality; we have little room or patience for the concept in our everyday sensory reality, the reality in which we mostly (in peacetime) live our lives. If our car breaks down inconveniently on a stormy night in the country, we might think of bad luck or evil forces, but know our real solution lies in a good repairman with his common sense, experience and technical skills. No matter what our hurry after the car is repaired, we would not drive our car over a child who has fallen off his bicycle and is lying in the street. This is the peacetime reality. We would, however, with no particular compunctions, bomb a city with ten thousand sleeping children in the reality picture of wartime perception. If we wish to understand what is going on here, we must not only look at the killing and willingness-to-kill of wartime, but how these are an integral part of a view of what perceived reality is and how it works. Reality is structurally different in the two views, and this difference leads inexorably to differences in thought and behavior and to a world where everything is black or white and there are no shades of grey. No important people in *Cinderella* are half good and half bad. The Stepmother and Stepsisters are all bad. Nothing that they think or do is good. Cinderella herself, the Fairy Godmother and the Prince are all good. Bad thoughts never cross their minds. When the two fated good ones, Cinderella and the Prince, meet, only good can result. And further, since they live in a reality where what they do now affects all of the future, "They live happily ever after." And in a war, we are good, they are totally bad.

The division of the world into the forces of Good

and the forces of Evil is so complete that not only similar qualities, but also similar actions by the two sides are seen as fundamentally different. The bombing of Coventry by the Germans and the bombing of Hamburg by the United States in World War II were seen as two different kinds of behavior. ("They did it first" and "You must fight fire with fire," as moral arguments belong in a schoolyard, not in any adult forum.)

It is clear that in these two situations, peace and war, we strongly tend to use different organizations of reality. From the other side of the coin we are in different states of consciousness.

This approach partially follows a lead developed by the biologist Johannes von Uexküll at the beginning of the 20th century. He showed that the physical organization of an organism, its sensory equipment, determined how it perceived the world. Further, that with different sensory equipment, different worlds were perceived by different organisms. In the world of the fly, he said, we see only "fly things," in the world of the sea urchin, only "sea urchin things."*

---

* "Uexküll once remarked that the formal structure (*Bauplan*) of each living being...enclosed this being as firmly as the walls of a prison. Nor does the human being escape this prison by destroying the walls: He escapes by being conscious of them. Here the Hegelian statement — that he who knows about a limitation is already free of it — holds true. This becoming aware is the beginning and the end, the alpha and the omega, of human freedom." (Ernst Cassirer, *The Logic of the Humanities*, Yale University Press, New Haven, 1961, p. 74.)

Human beings are not only constrained by their sensory equipment, but (as Ernst Cassirer has shown in such detail) also by the symbolic ways in which they organize and construe the world. When we are in the world of the dream and have built a world picture of one special sort, we perceive only "dream things." When we are in the world of the senses, as when we are driving our car in traffic, we perceive only "sensory things."

> Realism does not exist. Everything is invention. Reality is not realistic. It's another school of theater, a style.
>
> — Eugène Ionesco[2]

The *organization* of Psmith's consciousness, its structure and dynamic, followed exactly the organization of the world picture he was using at that moment. When playing chess the future is paramount and all thoughts and action are in terms of it. In erotic arousal or red rage the overwhelming intensity of the present fills consciousness and the future plays a very small, if any, part of it. We are not pretending or acting as if they do not exist. When Psmith was praying, numeration and counting did not exist for him. They had no part in the world picture he was using and therefore no part in his consciousness. The present and the future did exist and were very real to him. He was actively praying in terms of them.

There was no one "real" structure and dynamic in Psmith's consciousness. There was one "most common" one. It was the world picture taught him by his culture as the "real," the "normal" one. In our description of Psmith's day we see it from the beginning — where he sat at home reading his newspaper. This was similar to the picture he probably had while driving home, having his lunch or chatting with his coworkers.

As we continue this investigation it will become increasingly clear that the structure of his world picture and the structure of his consciousness were isomorphic — structurally identical. Which came first does not seem to be a fruitful question at this time.

We organize our perceived universe — including our sensory input, our needs and ourselves into a coherent whole. This is, at this moment, both "reality" and what we are. We shift this organization, this world picture into another — often a very different one — usually with such ease and flexibility that we are unaware of the change.

In the 16th century an American Indian, according to a story by Voltaire, wandered into a building of the Inquisition in Spain. He saw people trying to convince others to change their statements about God, and the others refusing, even in the face of torture and death. The Indian was puzzled by both groups of people. Why, he wondered, should one group want to change the statements of another on this subject, and why should the second group refuse?

It is clear that the Indian and the Spaniards described, perceived, and reacted to reality quite differently. The members of the Inquisition and their victims saw an eternity of afterlife as real and the most important part of reality and their present behavior as determining how they would spend it. Their viewpoint was clear: a short period of pain was as nothing compared to an eternity of bliss or torment. The Indian did not see this as a part of reality and so was completely confused by their behavior. Both the Indian and the Spaniards stood on the same portion of the earth, under the same sky, breathed the same air, and lived in quite different pictures of reality. Each culture had taught its members to perceive reality in a certain way and felt and deeply believed that its way led to the truth, that there was one "normal," "correct" world picture and it was theirs.

The sociologist Peter Berger uses the example of three different individuals who have the same dream. A deceased grandfather forces them to eat large quantities from a revolting dish. One says, "I had better stop eating heavy food in the evening." Another says, "I think I will call my psychoanalyst." The third says, "I wonder what my grandfather is trying to tell me." Each of these people clearly lives in a different world. In the first, one should stay healthy by listening to messages from the body. In the second, it is possible to get information from the subconscious. In the third, one ought to stay in touch with ancestors. Each of these individuals has an organized, coherent, valid world picture, an intelligible metaphysical system, although he may not have verbally elaborated it into a psycho–physiological theory of digestion, a psychoanalytical theory of dreams or a cosmology in which the living and the dead are both equally real and continue to interact. Each is a part of a general world picture shared with other members of their subculture.*

A father and son today discussing what the son should do now that he has finished high school might well face a similar situation. In the father's reality the son should go on to college, work hard, learn a skill or profession, find a useful place in the culture he lives in, get married, amass enough worldly goods so that he can live comfortably and safely, and make a contribution to society in a way that will be both useful to others and help to maintain the society that supports him. In the son's reality, he should take time to find out who he really is — what he likes and dislikes, what aptitudes he has, and what style most truly reflects his own personality — and seek a life that most gardens and grows his own unique being. In this reality, safety, happiness, and the best life come from internal harmony and from harmony between his natural style and his behavior, rather than from outside factors such as safe and approved work, insurance policies, and the like. Again, we have here two general world pictures, shared with many others during large portions of their lives.

---

* The study of the general world picture is far from new. Dilthey called them "World Views," Whitehead "Climates of Opinion," Durckheim "Collective Representations," Karl Popper "World Three," Ervin Laszlo, the most important worker in the field today "Cultural Cognitive Maps." (Peter Berger, *A Rumor of Angels*, New York: Doubleday, 1969, p. 71.)

...all perceptions, as well of the sense as of the mind, are according to the measure of the individual and not according to the measure of the universe. And the human understanding is like a false mirror, which, receiving rays irregularly, distorts and dissolves the nature of things by mingling its own nature with it.

— Francis Bacon, *The Idols of the Tribe*[3]

One night when my daughter was four years old, she called me after she was in bed. She had a nightlight but told me that she was frightened of the dark. I tried to reassure her and told her that there was nothing in the dark to be frightened of. She replied, "I'm not afraid of your dark. I'm afraid of my dark."

It was a powerful statement and jolted me. Wendy and I immediately arranged to leave the hall light on and her door partly open. With this she slept peacefully for some months and then, herself, asked to have the door closed.

What did her statement mean? Wendy and I sat in the same room at the same time, but clearly perceived the situation very differently. We had separate but overlapping sets of ideas as to how-things-are-and-work and therefore perceived the room and the world we were in in very different ways. A few examples of the different ways children and adults tend to perceive reality (in the particular subculture most of us tend to share at any rate) follow.*

---

* It should be stated here that the general world picture (GWP), those aspects of a world picture shared most of the time by the

In the child's world	*In the adult's world*
1. Everything revolves around me. If anything serious occurs, it is due to my thoughts or actions.	The world is not personal and does not revolve around me.

members of a group, is very close to the use of the term "culture" by anthropologists. There are many specific definitions of culture used in anthropology (see, for example, "When: A Conversation About Culture," Borovsky, Barth, Schweder, Rodseth and Stolzenberg, *American Anthropologist*, 103(2) 432-436, June 2001). However, Robert Redfield's 1941 "Shared Understandings Made Manifest in Act and Artifact" will probably do to show this relationship. (Robert Redfield, *The Folk Culture of Yucatan,* Chicago: University of Chicago Press, 1941.)

The GWP presents an image of what members of the culture agree is "reality." In many specific instances (e.g., Psmith) they believe and act according to another world picture, but faced with the problem, they will usually agree that reality is what the GWP says that it is.

The evolution and development of GWPs has been most profoundly studied by Ervin Laszlo and the World Futures General Evolution Group and the Academy for Evolutionary Development in Fuldar, Germany. Their work has been largely published by Gordon and Breach.

Alfred Korzybski, particularly in his *Science and Sanity,* has repeatedly pointed out the crucial fact that as long as a map is regarded as the territory it represents, much information is lost. Cognitive maps, world pictures, always miss much.

2. I can never be sure of anything. Things can change without notice. The world is full of surprises. What gets one result sometimes at another time gets a different result.

There is a consistency in the world even if I do not fully understand it. I can figure out general rules and thus predict events accurately.

3. The world is qualitative with feeling tone and emotion making up the most important aspects of reality. Thoughts and feelings cannot be separated from events.

The world is basically quantitative with things and quantities making up the most important aspects of reality. Thoughts and feelings are separate from events.

4. Variations in feelings (and therefore the color and shape of reality) are extreme. I feel completely safe or completely frightened.

There are many variations in feeling. There are mild, moderate and extreme states of all emotions.

The world that a child perceives and reacts to is a very different world than that of an adult from the same subculture. Not recognizing this fact makes communication ineffective, to say the least. It would have been pointless for me to keep telling Wendy that there was nothing to be afraid of in the dark. There was in her dark. That great philosopher Ernst Cassirer came into the bedroom of his daughter Anna when she was frightened and called him. In response to her explanation, he looked under the bed and told her that there were no lions there. She could not understand why everyone thought her father was so brilliant and intelligent when he did not know that as soon as he came into the room the lions went back to the zoo![4]

There are many ways of constructing reality, of conceiving how-things-are-and-work. Trying to communicate with someone who is using a different world picture than you are and not being aware of this will lead only to confusion.

> And the wildest dreams of Kew are the facts of
>   Khatmandhu,
> And the crimes of Clapham chaste in Martaban.
>
> — Rudyard Kipling[5]

II.
Consciousness and World Pictures

When you change the way you look at things,
the things you are looking at change.
— *Max Planck*

Inextricably enfolded with everything is our consciousness. Whether we see or hear, hope or dread, remember or foretell, the objects of our mental actions are so mixed with our consciousness we have no means of separating one from another. We can no more envision what is "out there" before it is mixed and synthesized with our consciousness and test our vision for validity, than we can imagine what our consciousness is before it is mixed and synthesized with whatever is "out there" and test our vision for validity.

When we try to look directly at our consciousness we find that it is transparent to our gaze. When we try to do experiments with it, we find that it is never the same at any two moments.

From the 1860s to the 1920s the structure and nature

of consciousness were the central focus and interest of psychology. Giants such as Wilhelm Wundt and Edward Bradford Titchener led a very large-scale foray into this area. In the 1920s interest began to turn elsewhere as we found no way to progress further or even to define our subject.

When I came into psychology in the late 1930s a major part of our history was the study of consciousness through introspection. Many of our academic parents had trained in this almost as hard and long as Zen monks. Much debate still continued on such topics as the differences about the existence of "imageless thought" of the Marburg and Würzburg schools.*

---

* This problem (imageless thought) has again today become one of academic interest. In recent years there has been a good deal of work on this question of the existence of pure thought. Forman's extensive survey of the field is important in understanding this work. Whether or not such a phenomenon exists is still a matter of debate. Forman and writers such as Stephen Katz come to opposite conclusions. (R.K.C. Forman, Ed., *The Problem of Pure Consciousness*, New York, Oxford University Press, 1990.)

I must confess that (probably due to my own poverty of imagination) I am unable to get my mind around the concept. For me a state of awareness without being aware of anything feels like a state of being in motion without changing position. However, people for whose work I have the greatest respect (including some outstanding Eastern savants) have been able to grasp the concept and believe it to be valid. The problem is an interesting one, although I am not clear about the implications of one conclusion or the other.

However, for the development of the taxonomy presented here I do not see any immediate relevance. I am dealing with mental processes after they have been alloyed with outside stimuli. These include, at the very least, the overwhelming content of our mental existence.

John B. Watson's viewpoint was being widely discussed and argued about in the 1930s and 1940s. Some psychologists and textbooks exulted that psychology was at last becoming a scientific discipline. Others argued that no real science ran away from its data and that studying psychology without consciousness was like ordering sirloin steak without meat. Many of our leaders saw Watson as the new Moses. Others believed that Behaviorism needed not a rebuttal but a cure.

Arguments were often heated. Reductionism and its validity were discussed then as much as they are now. In a panel at a major conference. Watson was advancing the idea that thought was "nothing but" miniscule movements of the voice box. The historian Will Durant disagreed strongly. In the middle of the debate Durant turned to the audience and said, "There is no point in continuing this discussion. It is obvious that Dr. Watson has already made up his larynx."[1]

The work of the Gestalt school, led by Wertheimer, Köhler and Köffka, was the elephant in the room that we all knew was there and did not know quite what to do with. We knew its importance but hoped that somehow it would stay in its place and remain limited to perception. It violated too many of our verbalized and unverbalized assumptions to be at all comfortable with. By and large we kept its strong and disturbing insights compartmentalized to visual perception and ignored their implications.

After 1920, over a period of twenty to thirty years,

the center of psychology shifted from the study of consciousness to the study of aspects of behavior that could be quantified. Whether you interpreted this as our field having finally shaken off the dusty shackles of philosophy or that psychology had lost its soul at its beginning and that it had now lost its mind, depended on your viewpoint. For my good or ill fortune, the psychology departments of the schools at which I studied (The College of William and Mary and the University of Chicago) were oases that remained somewhat aloof from the conflict and tried to see the best in both sides. I feel very fortunate in this happenstance.

Looking back at my own work during the last sixty-plus years I see how this early orientation has remained with and influenced me. The great majority of my publications have dealt with both consciousness and behavior. Whether I was writing on the similarities and differences of the structures of thought of mediums, mystics and physicists, or on body-mind medicine or on the thought processes of the SS during the Holocaust, the basic orientation remained.

I never attempted to actually define consciousness and it is only in the past few years that I have begun to face up to the problem. G.T. Ladd, one of the major psychologists of the time, wrote in 1887 in his classic *Psychology*, that although consciousness cannot be defined, its meaning can be brought out by contrast.

> What we are when we are awake, as contrasted to what we
> are when we sink into a profound and perfectly dreamless
> sleep, or as we swoon slowly away....[2]

Why we felt that we could not progress beyond this and what we could do about the problem has only begun to be a little clear to me in the past fifteen or so years.

To my knowledge, the first modern use of the word "consciousness" as an abstract concept was made in 1690 by John Locke in his *Essay Concerning Human Understanding*. He defined it as "the perception of what passes in a man's mind." Thereby he set the pattern, in the West, for the study of consciousness by looking inward. (The East had long embraced this approach.) This way of studying consciousness, even though it fits the common sense idea that if you wish to understand something you look at it, has not led to fruitful results.

Modern attempts to study and classify consciousness largely started in the 18th century with Kant, who distinguished between three aspects — cognition, affection and will. This influenced much of the work afterwards and was widely used. (When I was a college student most introductory textbooks in psychology still were divided into separate sections, one for each of the three aspects.) In the long run, however, it led to a dead end. Not only was there the fact that no one had ever seen a pure example of any of them, it was also true that when you attempted to work with the concept it proved to be unfruitful; it did not increase our understanding of ourselves.

Wilhelm Wundt, generally regarded as the father of experimental psychology, followed Locke's lead when he laid down the idea that all scientific study of consciousness is primarily done by looking within. "All psychology begins with introspection," he wrote in 1860. This was the start of a major sixty-year effort to analyze consciousness and classify the results by examining one's own inner processes.

Edward Bradford Titchener at Cornell led a large and influential school of American psychologists. His highly trained students spent thousands of hours in introspection. They, and many others in different laboratories, tried to find the elements of consciousness and classify them. For them, when an experience could not be dissected further, it was called "elemental."

The introspectionists such as Titchener, Wundt, Kulpe, Marbe, Ach, Watts and many others had thought that they could overcome the problems by rigorous training. In the event, however, they could not, they were unable to solve the problems of how to set up a classification system of consciousness by looking within. The multiple difficulties in this area proved insuperable.

In spite of this gigantic effort in many countries by hundreds of dedicated men and women, by 1920 it was generally agreed in psychology that the attempt was hopeless — that the elements of consciousness could not be identified and classified — and the work was abandoned.

After a lifetime of work in the field of consciousness, Titchener declared in 1929 that the subject of his work could not even be defined. All attempts before this (and since!) at formal definition were failures.

I know of no more successful definition in the hundred-plus years plus since then.

In the late 1800s Franz Brentano summarized "the most notable classifications of mental phenomena that have been made in the history of psychology."[3] These included the work of Aristotle, who classified mental phenomena into those that are and those that are not connected with bodily processes, those that are shared with animals and those that are not, and a third category. This one classified phenomena according to the object of their "intention." Thus, in a judgment something is being accepted or rejected, in an idea something is the focus of the idea, in love something is loved, and so forth. Hobbes in *The Leviathan* distinguished unguided, inconstant mental activity from that which is regulated by desire or design. Spenser and Bain divided mental processes into primitive and derivative.

Aristotle's category of "intention" very probably led to Kant's classification of cognition, affection, and will. This viewpoint ran through psychology at that time. G.F. Stout expressed it in his influential *A Manual of Psychology* in 1899, writing, "There are three ways in which our consciousness is related to an object ... knowing, feeling and striving."

The next major approach was that of Freud, who

classified the parts of the mind into ego, id and super-ego. Although this classification was viewed by many as a useful one — just as Kant's cognition, affection, and will had seemed many years before — in the long run it did not prove fruitful and is now for most psychologists mainly a matter of historical interest.

These and other classification systems were developed and worked with by psychologists and philosophers who recognized the great need for such a system. None of them proved useful. None of them led to further advances.

It *is* legitimate to say, "Let us make a metaphor. Let us see what happens if we describe the mind as if it were made up of three separate but interacting parts." Does the metaphor lead us to increased empathy for others? Or to a new comprehension of the inner life? Or to a new testable hypothesis? Is this triad a *fruitful* metaphor? This is a far cry from saying, "The mind is divided into three parts. They are cognition, affection and will, or ego, id and superego." This is also true of metaphors such as "The mind functions as if it were a machine." (Machine models included Carlisle's steam engine and Freud's hydraulic pump.) Or as if it were a flowering plant, a white rat writ large or a computer. These — as others — have been tried many times. Again, none has proved useful. Tempting as it is to say that consciousness functions in the same way as whatever is salient in the culture at a particular time (today, of course, a computer), experience has shown it does not help. Consciousness is unique. Metaphors only cloud our thinking.

Further, as has been pointed out repeatedly in philosophy, a definition or description is made in relation to other entities or processes in the same class. A tree is tall in relation to a bush, small in relation to a mountain. A rainbow is multicolored compared to the blue sky. These are comparisons. To what entity or process can we compare consciousness? What else is in the same class?

Even as psychologists and philosophers struggled for centuries to make progress in investigating consciousness, they had been warned that the methods they were using and the very definition of the object of their research was problematic.

All of the classifications they used, for example, were based on the idea that a science must directly observe its phenomena, that we must look within to develop a psychology. The problems with this in the study of consciousness were recognized early. Kant, in 1786, stated that psychology could never rise to the rank of an experimental science because "psychological observation interferes with its own object." G.G. Stokes, a noted mathematician and physicist of the period, said about psychology in his 1869 presidential address to the British Association for the Advancement of Science:

> Science can be expected to do but little to help us here since the instrument of research is itself the object of investigation; the mind which we study is the mind by which we study.[4]

William James (as usual) proceeded directly to one

aspect of the heart of the matter. In his 1912 *Essays in Radical Empiricism* he stated that consciousness is "the name of a non-entity." It is, he wrote, not a term, but a relation between two terms in which one *knows* the other.[5]

The present situation was bluntly stated in 1994 by N. Block, an authority on the subject. After describing the extensive research on the problems of thought, he wrote:

> ...in the case of consciousness we have nothing — zilch — worthy of being called a research program, nor are there any substantive proposals about how to go about starting one... Researchers are stumped.[6]

> Consciousness is a fascinating but elusive phenomenon: it is impossible to specify what it is, what it does or why it evolved. Nothing worth reading has been written about it.
> — *The International Dictionary of Psychology*, 1989

> When we look closely, it is not at all clear what the problem of consciousness actually is, and what we would accept as a convincing answer...where there are lingering mysteries in physics, chemistry and biology it is at least clear what would be accepted as a solution to the problem. This is not so for the problem of consciousness.
> —Thomas Metzinger[7]

Examples such as these statements of despair about the field of consciousness studies could be multiplied.

One more will suffice here however. Those two very high level researchers, Nobel Laureate Brian Josephson and Dr. Beverly Rubik, wrote in 1992:

> Despite the great practical importance of consciousness, science has as yet made little headway in understanding the phenomenon or even in deciding what it is.[8]

Of all the material I have read in this field, the most personally rewarding was *Science and Poetry* by Mary Midgley.[9] The voyage she invites the reader on is deep and wise, profound and stimulating and, to use a modern phrase, very reader friendly.

The exact definition of consciousness has been worked on in recent years by some of our best and most dedicated explorers. One need only to look at a paper such as Max Velman's excellent 2009 "How To Define Consciousness — And How Not To Define Consciousness"[10] to get some idea of the amount of serious work that has been done in this area. For those working in the field an interesting experience may be had by reading Christian de Quincey's 2006 "Switched on Consciousness"[11] and the comments on his paper by Michael Beaton, Jonathan Bricklin, Louis C. Charles, Jonathan C. W. Edwards, Ilya Farber, Bill Faw, Rocco J. Gennaro, Christian Kaernbach, Chris Nunn, Jaak Panksepp, Jesse Prinz, Matthew Ratcliffe, J. Andrew Ross, Murray Shanahan, Henry Stapp, and Douglas Watt. All of these are extremely competent researchers well familiar with the immense literature. There are basic differences between their approaches, viewpoints and conclusions. Much to my dismay I find myself nodding in agreement with all of them!

In science today we have given up the attempt to define the *fundamentals* of our universe or to find reasons for their existence. We know gravity by its relation to falling bodies, the orbits of planets and, perhaps, to distortions in the metric of space. We know inertia in its relation to mass and motion. We no longer try to define what matter is or what energy is. We look instead for the *effect* of their observables on each other.

When Clerk Maxwell, surely one of the greatest intellects in the history of physics, applied the "What is...?" question to matter and energy, he ended with:

> We are acquainted with matter only as that which may have energy communicated to it from other matter and which may, in its turn communicate energy to other matter.
>
> Energy, on the other hand, we know only as that which, in all natural phenomena, is continually passing from one portion of matter to another.[12]

Linnaeus nowhere struggled with the precise definition of life or living. He proceeded to classify its manifestations. Similarly Lord Kelvin spent a long and fruitful professional life in the study of matter. He never attempted to define his subject matter.

There are certain things that you simply cannot do,

and one saves a great deal of time and energy by learning what they are and stop trying to do them. Very few of us today spend much time trying to invent a perpetual motion machine that will do work or trying to determine the velocity and position of an electron at the same time or finding a definite end to the definition of *pi*.

There is an important impossibility which we have not fully accepted as such: it is to define what consciousness *is*. It is very hard to conceive of consciousness in its pure form, before it is alloyed with stimuli from whatever is outside of itself. In any case, at least the largest part of our consciousness seems to be open to our perception and analysis only after this synthesis.

When serious people study an area for a long period of time and end with conclusions like these, we can be reasonably sure that there is an assumption or a group of assumptions in their work blocking their progress. A basic and critical assumption running all through research and theory in this field is that consciousness has a stable and describable structure and/or dynamic. This assumption — and it is only that — apparently has been taken from our experience with physical things, from our observations of Descartes' *res extensa*. In spite of our long acceptance of this assumption there is no reason to believe it is valid.

Since the Enlightenment view of reality swept the Western world starting in the 17th century, it has generally been believed that if reason were properly applied we could find "clear and distinct ideas" in every realm of experience. On these we could build a science. "We hold these truths to be self-evident..." wrote Thomas Jefferson. These "self-evident," "clear and distinct ideas" could, it has been believed, serve us as axioms as they served Euclid. In the field of consciousness we have not been able to find such ideas.

In this field there have been assumptions that something that does not exist in space as we know it, that cannot be observed, that is composed only of processes, that is not quantitative in nature and that offers only private access, can be studied in the same ways or similarly defined as the other entities which science studies. The astronomer Sir Arthur Eddington put it forcefully:

> To those who have any acquaintance with the laws of chemistry and physics, the suggestion that the world [of consciousness] could be ruled by laws of allied character is as preposterous as the suggestion that a nation could be ruled by laws like the laws of grammar.[13]

The special problems inherent in studying consciousness may be considered under three artificially separated headings. The combination of these three aspects has appeared to be an insuperable obstacle.

1. From the beginning of science we have known that if we wished to understand more about something we should observe it and/or its effects. In the realm of consciousness we have been unable to do this. Consciousness itself is trans-

parent to our gaze. We can observe the object of its actions and the attendant feeling tone we have towards the object — what we are loving or hating or judging or desiring and how strongly we feel about it — but not consciousness itself. Using consciousness to view consciousness has not been possible: the instrument can see anything but itself. From Kant on we have always viewed this as a major obstacle to a scientific investigation of consciousness.

Nor have we fared better in studying the effects our consciousness produces. Except in the area of the *correlations* between physiological and conscious events (when the body drinks, the mind also gets drunk), we have been unable to study this area or even to define it. Whether we theoretically separate matter and mind as did Descartes into *res extensa* and *res cogitans*, or we theoretically bring them together and consider them as aspects of a larger One, the result is the same. We appear to find ourselves blocked at every turn. Even when we focus on the effects of consciousness on the brain (as when a Yogi deliberately slows his brain waves as registered on a machine) we get no closer to understanding consciousness itself.

Events in consciousness and events in the physical brain resemble each other (in Sir Arthur Eddington's phrase) "as much as do a telephone number and a subscriber." Between them there appears to be (in another famous phrase) "a bridge of cobwebs a mile long." We have been unable to conceive of a way to cross this theoretical bridge.

Changes in the brain are frequently followed by changes in consciousness and vice versa. That has been all (except for details) that we have been able to confidently state. Neither a reductionist approach nor systems theory has appeared to help us very much. Nor has anything else.

2. The second major obstacle has been the nature of the observables which we find in this realm. There are no separate entities but rather a kaleidoscopic field of interacting processes which are never still, never repeated. (The idea of a mental state being repeated is, said William James, "as mythical as the Jack of Spades."[14]) Further, mental states change as we try to look at them. If I want to know what an angry person is like and look within myself the next time I am angry, I immediately am no longer an angry person, but an observing person.

Compounding this problem is the fact that the observables are, in principle, non-quantitative. For quantitative assessment public access to the data is required. (You and I and Dick and Harry must *all* be able to look at the same data.) Consciousness has only private access. You and I cannot agree on how many units of pain your gallstone is giving you or what a unit of pain represents. We have *names* for units of consciousness but that is all. The unit of joy is an "exuberant," the unit of pain is a "dol" (from *dolor*), and the unit of love a "Romeo." But how much pain a dol represents is an impossible question to answer. There is no way to determine if your dol of pain is the same as mine. All attempts at quantification of events in consciousness have ended in hopeless failure.

3. The third obstacle, clearly deriving from the other two, has been the lack of a classification system of the aspects or of the types of consciousness. In science we have known, since Linnaeus at any rate, that until we have an adequate way of classifying our data we cannot think clearly about it. The famous statement that Linnaeus "found biology a chaos and left it a cosmos"[15] describes well the state of the field before and after his classification system.

In the realm of consciousness, all attempts at classification systems have failed.

The reasons usually given for the difficulties in the study of consciousness are the ones we have described so far. However, although these are true and important statements of the problems, there is also a deeper, a more profound and hidden problem in studying consciousness. This is that, from a scientific point of view, such questions as "What is the pure structure of consciousness?" and "What is the structure and dynamic of consciousness before it is affected by outside reality?" are invalid questions. From the viewpoint of scientific methodology, an invalid question is one that in principle cannot be answered and *the answer tested for truth or falsity.*

Before its integration with outside-of-it-reality, consciousness cannot be observed and cannot be dealt within a thought experiment. We simply cannot conceive of its parts or structure in a way that can be tested for validity. Similarly, reality outside of consciousness, as Einstein said, is a "sealed watch." We cannot conceive of its form in such a way that we can test our conception. As Einstein and Infeld observed, if we say that reality without the integration with consciousness is such and such, and we now plan to test the truth or falsity of our description, the second part of the statement would have no meaning.[16] In Percy Bridgeman's terms, there are no operations we can perform to make this test except verbal ones. In science we have learned that purely verbal proofs are insufficient unless they can be made to rest on observation. Here this cannot be done in principle. There is no possible way to "observe" reality without using consciousness. Similarly there is no possible way to observe consciousness without reality. To conceive of consciousness alone is, as J. N. Findley wrote, to have a "series of cogitative flashes in which nothing whatever was cogitated or symbolized."[17]

There is no implication here that reality-outside-of-consciousness does not exist. What *is* said here is that any question about this by itself cannot be answered *and the validity of the answer tested* in principle, and therefore it is an invalid question from a scientific viewpoint. A science cannot be built on invalid questions. *If we wish to have a science of consciousness we must build it on questions which can be answered. Since we cannot, in principle, separate "consciousness" from "external reality," we must study the synthesis produced by the two.*

We have been asking an invalid question: "What is the structure of consciousness itself?" To this we have found no fruitful answer nor will we be able to do so. However, there are questions which we *can* ask.

We *can* ask: "What are the forms that appear *after* the integration of consciousness and outside reality?" "What different structure and sets of dynamics do we find *after* the synthesis?" These forms are organized by us into wholes which can be called world pictures. A world picture is an organized set of beliefs about how-things-are-and-work. It has a structure and a dynamic which can be described. It is a conception of reality. It answers questions such as those of Kant: "What can I know" "What ought I to do?" "What dare I hope?" "What is a human being?" In the description of Psmith's day in the previous chapter we saw Psmith use a number of very different pictures.

Every world picture is a *coherent* construction of the total cosmos including the self and definitions of time, space, causation and identity. The picture involves goals, hopes and fears. What one worships and how and at what one laughs. How one sits, stands and weeps. How one relates to oneself, others and the universe. What is flexible and negotiable in life and what is not. How many kinds of love, snow, Gods, death, success, camels, reality and stages of life are differentiated.

Finely or broadly articulated, we each, at each moment, have a world picture. Generally we are not aware of what it is, but it is always present and determines much of what we perceive and how we act. We *can* ask: "What world pictures are formed by the interactions of consciousness and outside-of-it-reality?" "How can we order and classify these world pictures?"

Since consciousness is an integral part of whatever world picture is being used at a particular moment *and follows the structure and laws of that world picture,* we are not only setting up a classification system of world pictures, but also one of aspects of and states of consciousness.

If I have at a particular moment a world picture in which will (executive decision-making ability) does not exist, I do not make any decisions. If I have a world picture in which a symbol is the same entity as the referent it stands for, then I will be as angry at the burning of the flag of my country as I will be if there is an active attack upon the country. If I have a world picture in which the future is of paramount importance and present actions inexorably determine the future — as in actively playing chess or doing long division, then I, my consciousness, will feel emotion about my present actions *only* as they determine the future. If the opposite is true — as in a red rage or in the height of erotic arousal — I am consciously concerned only with the present.

To study consciousness in this manner, we first ask in what ways, along what parameters, do our various world pictures differ? In some, for example, the individual has the ability to make decisions and act on them, in some he does not. In some, as the one we use in a dream state, anything clearly conceived of is real. In others, as the one we use when working in a chemistry laboratory, only things that have consistent effects on other things are real.

We can classify world pictures in terms of where they are on these parameters. For example, we can say of a particular worldview that will is present (is an observable in this state), that anything conceived of is real, and so on through all the parameters we have defined. We can thus order and classify aspects of consciousness and states of consciousness in the same way that Linnaeus classified and ordered biological entities. We now have the basis for a science of consciousness.

The roots of this approach go back to Vico,[18] von Herder,[19] James,[20] and others. It could not have been developed before the revolution in physics which occurred in the early 20th century. Henry Margenau and the present writer have described the reasons for this in some detail in our book *Einstein's Space and Van Gogh's Sky*.[21]* Suffice it to say here that until science realized that quantum physics presented a valid picture of reality, of how-things-are-and-work very different from that presented by the senses, and that the same thing was true of relativity physics, we were not free to proceed with a science of consciousness. The concept that these world pictures were equally valid, very different and yet compatible, opened new doors.[22]

Vico's Children

The real background of this work started with the

---

* In quantum mechanics, "The motion of the smallest particles was shown to be subject to the laws of large numbers. Any individual instance showing evidence of intractable caprice..." (H. Morgenthau, *Thomas and the Physics of 1958*, Milwaukee: Marquette University Press, 1958.) This marked the end of the theory that the universe was everywhere consistent and that there existed somewhere a world picture or equation that would include everything.

New Science of Giambattista Vico in the 18th century. Here for the first time in human history a specific and clear statement was made. This was that there are different, equally valid ways of organizing our sensory input: that they lead to different possibilities and impossibilities. Thus, Vico pointed out, *Hamlet* could not have been written in Homer's time nor *The Iliad* in Shakespeare's. Neither is superior to or more valid than the other, they are just different.

One did not develop out of another and is therefore superior to it any more than a saw developed out of a hammer and is therefore "higher." World pictures are tools, each adapted to specific types of problems and needs and using different methods.

New refinements may have developed as Descartes refined one method and the Philokalia and the Vedas another.

Vico's work was largely ignored in his lifetime. Later in the 18th century von Herder picked it up and applied it to different cultures. He stressed that each had a different "center of gravity" and their world pictures varied widely, leading to completely different sets of problems and developments. Thus, we might say today, very few people had an identity crisis or "middle age crisis" in the Medieval periods, and very few go through a thorough ego-shaking "crisis of faith" in ours. Although Vico's insights became widely known and influenced a number of our intellectual leaders, the implications of those insights have been very little accepted. We read William James'

Varieties and his *Pluralistic Universe*, Ernst Cassirer's *Symbolic Forms* and Isaiah Berlin's *Vico and Herder* and think well of them and do not change our thinking at all.

The trouble is we have a basic commitment to the idea that there is one true, valid concept of reality (ours, of course) and that all others are primitive, childlike, mythological or pathological.

Generally speaking the cultural anthropologists (there are, of course, exceptions like Mead, Benedict, Malinowski, Greenfield and others) genuflect and pay lip service to the idea that a native tribal view of reality is valid with their prejudices to the contrary shining through at every pore.

The anthropologist, and practically everyone else east and west, believes in his heart that one of two things about reality is true. The first is that reality "really is" what our sensory array tells us it is. The desk we lean on *is* hard and brown, and Eddington's other desk, made up of "empty space haunted by areas containing mass, charge and velocity" is also real, but our feelings tell us its reality lies somewhere between that of Washington's cherry tree and the Easter Bunny. (And never mind Hiroshima and Nagasaki.)

The other set of beliefs that is widely spread over the human race is that reality comes in two editions — trade and deluxe. Here are Plato's appearances and forms, Kant's phenomena and noumena, the Buddhist illusion and Brahma and a very wide selection of others. All agree that both editions are real, but the deluxe is somehow more real (sort of like Orwell's *Animal Farm,* in which all the animals were equal but some were more equal than others).

We today see and largely ignore the current flowing from Vico's brilliance except for a few theoretical physicists who have only rarely heard of Vico. These physicists have learned from Max Planck and Einstein how fundamentally different reality in the micro-universe is from reality in the sensory universe and in the macro-universe. They accept this in their work but most of them are fundamentally and emotionally committed to there being only one real picture of reality, and they stay on the quest for a unified field theory to explain and connect these different world pictures.

By and large we have ignored the hard core of Vico's work, that there is no way to rank the great world pictures on a validity scale except in terms of specific goals. The approach presented here is that to ask the question "What is the true shape of reality?" is meaningless. (In science, as we all are aware, a meaningless question is one that you cannot, even in theory, answer and prove your answer's validity.) We *can* ask: "In order to attain a particular goal what is the best way to construe reality, the best way for our specific purposes?" To go further than this is, as Max Planck pointed out, a matter for religion, not science.

Each species has a sensory array that gives it a specific world picture. This is the world picture that makes it most likely that the species will survive (its alpha world picture).

The framework presented here is one step in the development of our understanding of what Ervin Laszlo and his associates (The World General Evolution Research Group) call cognitive maps. Laszlo and others have been studying this area for some time now, and their careful intensive and extensive work is, I believe, essential if we wish to further increase our understanding of consciousness. For anyone interested in this I highly recommend their series of books *The World Futures General Evolution Studies.*[23]

Further, what we can conceptualize, say or communicate in one world picture, we often cannot in another. Each has different possibilities. The French philosopher Gabriel Marcel was speaking to a group of American philosophers about grace and transcendence. They kept interrupting him with, "Dr. Marcel, define your terms." "What do you mean by that?" Finally Marcel replied, "I see I cannot define it in your terms, but if I had a piano here I could play it for you."

This "Eternity" is neither shorter nor longer than "a billion years." The two terms refer to different classes of world pictures and simply do not relate to each other.

"... as Mach, Duhem, and Poincaré observed, an indefinite number of explanations applies to any set of observations."[24]

This viewpoint is the logical extension of the great revolution in physics that occurred in the beginning of the 20th century. Of this, Louis de Broglie wrote "The scientific method had become visible, and science could no longer report on an independently existing world." Niels Bohr put it that since then, "It is wrong to think that the task of physics is to find out how nature is." Werner Heisenberg said that physics had learned to change the usual words "interpretation of nature" to "description of nature." With the new understanding, wrote Heisenberg, reality "evaporates." Hans Vaihinger wrote:

> It must be remembered that the object of the world of ideas as a whole is not the portrayal of reality — this would be an utterly impossible task — but rather to provide us *an instrument for finding our way about more easily in this world* (italics his). Subjective processes of thought inhere in the entire structure of cosmic phenomena.[25]

And yet, it is not a new concept. There is a story by Voltaire about a being from Jupiter who visits Earth. He belongs to a race that lives for thousands of years and has seventy-two senses. They have been deeply devoted all through their history to the study of truth. At the end of his visit he gives a gift to the Earth philosophers. It is a book, he says, that tells everything that can be known about ultimate reality. All of its pages are blank.

No truly human characteristics can be described in any world picture that has quantitative aspects. Those observables which make us uniquely human, including compassion, love, loyalty, courage — those characteristics which in Plato's words, "keep us on two legs instead of four" — and which no machine could ever have. None of these can be measured quantitatively. This fact, which psychologists have found very hard to accept, has been widely understood by the artist. The poet Lawrence Binyón wrote:

> For Mercy, Courage, Kindness, Mirth,
> There is no measure upon Earth.
> Nay, they wither root and stem
> If an end be set to them.[26]

With this in mind let us see where the idea of a classification system of world pictures leads us.

III.
The First Classification System:
The Realms of Consciousness

Classification of things into extensive "kinds" is
thus the first step: and classification of their relations
and conduct into extensive "laws" is the last step,
in their philosophic unification.
— *William James*

It is a principle of scientific reasoning that if two things
cannot be separated or differentiated so that they have
different effects, they are to be considered to be one
thing. A state of consciousness and its corresponding
world picture cannot be separated and they cannot be
differentiated except artificially — heuristically.

I have written here that the world picture includes
the person who holds it and is defined by it, that any
separation of the person and the world picture is an invalid one. The concept that knower and known are one
is a very old one, dating at least to St. Thomas Aquinas
in the 13th century. It may be worth noting here that the

general approach of this book is in agreement with the viewpoint of Thomas Aquinas in many respects and differs sharply in others.

The agreements include:

1. The union between the knower and known. In the words of Jacques Maritain: "For Aquinas to know is to become… no type of material union or transformation can attain to the degree of union between the knower and the known…. The union of the knower and the known is a…genuine unity; they are more than matter and form joined together."[1]

2. Human beings exist in different universes according to the way that they define reality. In the Thomist view Man is situated by his very existence at the juncture of different universes. In Aquinas' words, "like a horizon of the corporeal and the spiritual."[2]

3. For Aquinas there were two separate kinds of knowledge. The first is acquired by observation and reason. It concerns facts and has nothing to do with moral values. The second is acquired through what Aquinas called "inclinations," through "sympathy, congeniality, co-naturality."

The second gives moral values, the knowledge of the mystic and the artist. The first must be approached intellectually and objectively. The second is subjective and interior. Neither can solve the problems of the other. Thus a man may know everything about values through the first kind of knowledge, but not be a virtuous man. But if he knows about them through the second kind, he is, in Aquinas' term, "co-natured" with them and therefore behaves virtuously.*

The disagreements include:

1. All kinds of knowledge agree if they are used correctly. For Thomas, the two kinds of knowledge must be in agreement since the first is of the works of God and the second comes from God.

2. You can legitimately use the same type of logic with all types of knowledge. For Aquinas, Aristotelian logic (Psmith working at his desk) could be used with both of the two types of knowledge he recognized. From the *Landscapes of the Mind* viewpoint, each Realm has its own definition of space, time, identity and causation, and thus inevitably its own logic.

3. All people, Aquinas believed, have within themselves and often unrecognized by them, the same moral values. Modern psychology and anthropology have long since overthrown this view.

---

* It is interesting to note that Aquinas speaks to the heart of this book when he wrote of "the factive intellect" (*intellectus agens*), which takes the sensory input and organizes it into coherent wholes. (*Summa Theol,* Gilby tr., 1.9.84.A6 and 1.9.55.A2.) To my knowledge this is the earliest statement of this concept.

Of major importance is the trend in psychology in the last century toward the understanding that the person and the environment cannot be separated in any meaningful way. In psychology and psychiatry one thinks particularly of Goldstein, Angyal, Lewin and Maslow. This understanding is present in fields other than psychology, of course. In biology one thinks of von Uexküll, in history of Robin Collingwood. In philosophy the idea goes back at least to Aquinas. Since Boas, the idea has been central in anthropology. In physics one thinks of the problems and insights of quantum mechanics.

In this present work I am saying that you cannot separate the person and the perceived environment since they mutually create one another. The environment of the person as it is perceived is reality for that person and it is to this environment that he reacts. The person exists and perceives himself as a part of this reality. At any moment they are two sides of the same coin.*

It is therefore logical that we set up a classification system of the parameters, the dimensions, in terms of which world pictures vary. This is also a classification

* It is not usual or popular (if indeed permitted!) in the social sciences today to quote historical figures such as Vico or Thomas Aquinas. However, when some of the greatest minds of our species have delved into the area you are exploring, it is hubris at least, and certainly stupidity as well, to ignore them and not to seriously consider their work and conclusions. Further, if you ignore the history and metaphysics — the philosophy — behind your thinking, then, as a great many unfortunate examples in the history of thought tell us, they are quite likely, sooner or later, to come around you and bite you on the behind!

system of aspects of consciousness and of states of consciousness, and opens the way for a science of consciousness. What Linnaeus did for biology it seems possible to do for consciousness: order and classify the observables in this realm of experience without losing any of the richness and vitality of our human existence.

World pictures can be separated into classes such as Kingdoms, Realms and Domains. Following Linnaeus, Kingdoms are the largest general classes into which the phenomena in a taxonomy are divided. In biology we have Animals and Plants (and lately several others) as the largest classes. Within these large classes all entities share certain characteristics. Within each of these general classes are smaller, more specific ones we will call Realms and Domains. (Under Animals are "Animals without backbones," and "Animals with backbones," for example.) *In a taxonomy of world pictures each Kingdom has its own definition of space, time, identity, causation, geometry and logic. Within each Kingdom are a number of Realms and Domains. All Domains in the same Realm share the same definitions of the basic factors, but differ from each other in specific ways.*[3]

Thus Christian, Mohammedan and Jewish fundamentalists might share the same beliefs as to how-the world-is-and-works, agree on the proper logic and geometry, and the proper way to reach truth and solve problems, etc., but disagree on such matters as whether the true scripture, the true presentation of *important* aspects of reality is in the Old Testament, the Old and the New Testaments, or both of these plus the Koran. Their world pictures are in the same Realm but in different Domains of that Realm. The principle holds true for most classification systems. No two trees are identical, nor are any two trees-with-leaves nor — as we go to finer and finer definitions — any two Silver Birches.

The classification system described here has taken elements from Linnaean biology and classification, *The Diagnostic and Statistical Manual of Mental Disorders*; *The International Classification of Diseases, Number 9*, (Clinical Modification) and the Dewey Decimal System. These are the very widely used classification systems today.

Most classification systems start with the largest possible natural groupings (Kingdoms), such as Plants and Animals in the older biology and then proceed in one way or another to the most specific classes identifying the individual as precisely as possible, i.e., Species, Homo sapiens.[4]

How shall this be done with world pictures? What are the largest natural groupings to be found?

(The fact that, as in Psmith's day, world pictures vary so widely and on so many parameters, makes the problem appear to be difficult to solve. Perhaps a little comfort can be taken from the fact that Linnaeus faced the need to devise a taxonomy that would include armadillos, wasps, jellyfish, redwood trees, giraffes, tigers, mushrooms, clams, condors, human beings and octopi, and he succeeded.)

I have, in this tentative first taxonomy for the equivalent in our work of Linnaeus' Plants and Animals begun with one criterion for these basic Kingdoms. Are the observables Quantitative or Non-quantitative?

In the Quantitative Kingdom everything that is real can be numbered. The basic statement is "everything that exists, exists in some quantity" and exact and precise numbers can be ascribed to it. I can say there are forty-three inches or twenty-one liters or three sonatas or 215 cats, and so forth.

In the Non-quantitative Kingdom precise numbers generally cannot be ascribed. We find questions such as, "How much do I love you?" "How much better a writer was Hemingway than Brontë?" (or vice versa, if you wish) and "How tall was the beanstalk that Jack climbed?"

> "Now it is the essence of mental things," wrote the philosopher Henri Bergson, "that they do not lend themselves to measurement"... You cannot have a ton of love (in spite of the way girls used to sign their letters) or a yard of hate or a gallon of numinous awe; but love and hate and awe are just as real as a ton of flour or a yard of linen or a gallon of petrol, more real indeed, because they have immediate significance. They are not simply means to ends like making bread, a pillow case or haste."[5]

In a Quantitative world picture I can describe my data in ever-finer terms. I can state that from the cannon to the target is so many miles or so many yards or so many feet or inches or thousandths of an inch or ten-thousandths of an inch and so on forever. In a world picture that is not quantitative, however, I can sometimes say that there are three bears or four princes but soon after that there are only "many" or "so many" soldiers that they "drink the rivers up" and "their shafts benight the air." In the myth the father flees the Elf-king through the cold night, but I cannot say that he rides at twelve and a half miles an hour in a temperature of twenty-seven degrees Fahrenheit. Some world pictures are quantitative, and some are not. This does not reflect in any way which ones are more "real." My love for you is as real as the box of candy I bring you, but I can describe one of these in the exact number of pieces in the box or in pounds and ounces or calories and not the other.

This quantitative criterion seems straightforward enough and a good beginning. However, when we try to use it in practice, we find it is too broad to deal with many problems. Very often we need another criterion — are events discrete and separate from each other as are fish and comets and shoes? Or do all the events and entities flow into each other as do pressure, temperature and volume of an enclosed gas so that they can no more be meaningfully separated than can the parts of our experience of ourself at any given moment? We must proceed from Kingdom to Realm.

In some world pictures objects and events are separate and affect each other by bumping into each other or by some other form of energy or information exchange.

This is true in the world-as-perceived-by-the-senses. The baseball is certainly affected by the pitcher and the catcher, but it is separate from both of them, and after the game all three may go their separate ways and cease to affect each other. In other constructions of reality this is not so. Entities and processes cannot be meaningfully separated from each other. This essential view of the cosmos is the "seamless garment" of the mystics in which "thou can'st not stir a flower without the troubling of a star." The physicist Herman Weyl wrote:

> For field-theory, a material particle such as the electron, is merely a small area of the electrical field in which the strength of the field assumes an enormously high value and where there is, consequently, an intense concentration of field force. This schema of the world reduces to a complete continuum.[6]

The world as seen in the construction given by relativity theory is such a complete continuum. Space and time in this world picture cannot be separated even though they are quantitative. All things flow into each other. This is true to the degree that the physicists Lev Landau and G.B. Rumer could write: "To say that two things occurred at the same place is as meaningless as saying that they occurred at the same time."[7] The world-view of relativity physics and that of some mystical states *cannot* be differentiated on the basis of the continuous nature of reality.[8] They *can* be differentiated on the basis that one contains a quantitative aspect in its world picture and the other does not.

This criterion — is it a Quantitative or Non-quantitative world picture and is it one in which entities are discrete or continuous — appears to be of major importance in setting up our new taxonomy.

To begin then, two Kingdoms and four Realms are defined. These are four classes into which, it seems at the present time, all world pictures will fit.

Table One *A Beginning Taxonomy of World Pictures*				
Kingdoms	K1 Quantitative		K2 Non-Quantitative	
Realms	K1i Quantitative Discrete	K1ii Quantitative Continuous	K2i Non-Quantitative Discrete	K2ii Non-Quantitative Continuous
Domains				

Table Two *The Realms of Experience*		
Number	Description	Example
i.	Quantitative/Discrete	The world picture of the human sensory array.
ii.	Quantitative/ Continuous	The world picture of field theory and relativity theory.
iii.	Non-Quantitative/ Discrete	The world picture of the myth, fairy tale, and dream.
iv.	Non-Quantitative/ Continuous	The world picture of cosmic consciousness and satori.

The first Realm— i — is the one in which events and entities are both quantitative and discrete. Dorothy's home in Kansas comes quickly to mind. We can, at least in theory, find out exactly and precisely how far is the way from the schoolhouse to Auntie Em's front porch and Dorothy; Auntie Em and Toto are all separate from each other. Psmith was a part of this world picture at his desk designing a new automotive drive train or when he was driving home in the traffic. As this is the Realm revealed by the human sensory array, it is the predominant — the alpha realm for human beings. The sensory apparatus of an organism is *an array of biological sensors which reveals the world picture essential to the biological survival of the species.* This includes the survival of the individual organism, at least until it reproduces. The environment of a species is determined by its sensory apparatus. This reveals its alpha world pictures.

For each species the environment provided by its sensory apparatus is "reality." What, for example, does "time" mean to a wood tick which can remain fastened to the underside of a branch without moving for at least seventeen years, then, when an organism smelling of perspiration is beneath it, will release its hold and fall on the prey?[9]

If there is any meaning to the term "reality," it is species specific. It is reality as perceived by the sensory apparatus of the species.

This reality given by the sensory array of a specific species is the predominant, the alpha definition of reality for that species. Survival of the organism and the species itself depends on this. For humans it is the world as revealed by our senses, the quantitative world in which entities are discrete, separate from each other. It is the world in which we have the technology to achieve results we wish. It is the world picture in which after the LSD trip or the vision quest or the Fourth of July celebration, we use a pot of water or a full bladder to put out our campfire and know that if we put one foot out after another in a certain way we can move across distance. And the technology in this world picture tells us that if we wish our belongings to come with us we must either carry them or put them on our horse or in our car.

Imagine if you can what sort of world picture your sensory array would give you if you could never see or touch any part of yourself, if you moved equally easily in three dimensions and if the third dimension (up and down) had a top to where you feel impelled to go every so often. Further, with all other moving objects you perceived the inside (hollows and solid areas in particular) as clearly as the outside. This is the input of the sensory array of the dolphin, and it is very hard for us as humans to conceive of the resultant alpha world picture.

The second Realm — ii — comprises those world pictures which are quantitative, but in which entities are not discrete, are not separate from each other. We can quantify the various forces in an electric field, but cannot separate them from each other. Or, in a container of gas, we can quantify volume, pressure, and temperature, but each of them is so determined by the others that none can change alone — they are continuous with each other. When Psmith, was at his desk working on an electrical network for a factory complex, he was in a quantitative/continuous world picture. The same was true when he was making and tasting his favorite and famed barbecue sauce by blending combinations of herbs until it was exactly right.

The third Realm — iii — is the one in which events and entities are non-quantitative and discrete. Oz comes to mind here. One cannot, in principle, find out precisely how long the Yellow Brick Road is or exactly how long Dorothy and the Scarecrow were together before they met the Tin Woodman, but all of them — girl, Scarecrow and Woodman — are separate from each other. When Psmith was praying on the stairs he was part of a world picture in this Realm, similarly later at night, asleep and dreaming, his world picture was in this Realm.

The fourth Realm — iv— is the one in which events and entities can neither be quantified nor separated from each other. Our own *experience* of our consciousness is one example of this. When we are in the kind of state of consciousness which we label cosmic consciousness or Christ consciousness or satori or such, the whole universe is constructed in this way: the universe is a seamless garment. When Psmith was dancing so well, he was part of a world picture in this Realm,

The four Realms appear, at this time, to be a useful way to begin building a taxonomy of world pictures. This would be a classification of constructions which would include our view of how-things-are-and-work (and our parallel state of consciousness) when we are dreaming, speeding down the incline of a roller coaster, administering CPR, threading a needle, solving an algebra problem, comforting a hurt child, listening to the Waldstein sonata with total concentration, experiencing the peak sexual moment, and many, many more. Hopefully these four Realms will include those and all of our other states of consciousness/world pictures.

IV.
The Realms of a World Picture

Whoever undertakes to set himself up as judge
in the field of Truth and Knowledge
is shipwrecked by the laughter of the gods.
— *Albert Einstein*

A Realm is basically defined by the characteristics of the observables found in it. Are they quantitative? Are they discrete? When we define Realms in this way we find that they each have specific laws (basic limiting principles). They differ in such things as the definition of space and of causation. Therefore before discussing these four classes of world pictures in more detail, we must first decide *how* to describe them. The following pattern seems to be fruitful.

1. The definition of real. What are the factors which make an entity or process something to be considered real in this Realm? This will include the definition of a valid source of information and a description of how we know if some-

thing is true. The valid road to truth and the decision as to what is real and what is not are inextricably bound together. (This category is placed first because, in practice, it seems to be felt by many people to be absolutely basic to their world picture. If you wish to turn an amiable discussion into an angry argument, question the other person's *methodology* for finding truth. Suggest to a scientist that the experimental method is limited to certain types of problems and has serious flaws when applied to others. Suggest to an orthodox Catholic that the Bible, like the Koran or Analects, is only one source of possible truths and that like all books it contains many errors. Ask any fundamentalist not what his or her scripture says or how it can be interpreted, but why *it* should be considered a source of *the* truth with so many competitors. Then duck!)

2. What entities are dealt with? What are the observables in this Realm? There are Realms which deal only with entities and events accessible to human senses, or deal with entities and events beyond the senses, too small or too large for the human sensory array even theoretically, and so forth.

3. What kind of algorithms (general processes, causal sequences, sequential chains) are used in this Realm? In some Realms these are Markovian — that is, each step inexorably and exactly follows the previous ones, as in doing long division. Free will does not exist. Everything is mechanically foreordained. In others they are non-Markovian — each step is a logical outcome of the past but could not have been

precisely predicted. We see this in the script of a theatrical play. Free will exists.

4. What kind of questions can and cannot be answered in this Realm? In some, as in the world picture revealed to our senses, one can answer "how" questions and some "what" questions, but not "why" questions. Various possibilities and combinations exist.

5. What are the definitions of space, time and energy in this Realm?

6. What is the geometry of this Realm?

It must be kept clear that each of these four classes of very different world pictures (and its corresponding state of consciousness) is powerful, valid and coherent. They are each valid for certain purposes, invalid for others. Each way is a great set of wings that help us to certain goals. When used to try to help us reach other goals, they do not work. Baudelaire wrote of the albatross soaring gracefully and expertly in the air. When brought down to a solid surface it is clumsy and inept. "Its giant wings keep it from walking."[1]

⁊

Realm i - The Quantitative/Discrete Realm

This is the Realm which deals with the world as it is perceived by the human senses. All real entities and events can be assigned numbers. Distances and times can be quantified as finely and precisely as needed. Thus in Dorothy's Kansas the distance from the schoolhouse to home can be described in miles, yards, feet, inches, thousandths of an inch, and so forth. Entities are separate and can be numbered from one to as many as exist: from the one elephant on the veldt to the number of atoms in the galaxy. Entities are discrete and interact through energy or information exchange. This is the Realm which the usual Western-raised and trained person would describe as common sense. It is the human alpha realm.

From the viewpoint of any specific species, the worldview given by its sensory array is its alpha world construction, it is the *true*, the real, picture of reality. Any species that does not act as if this were so ceases to exist. (There will, of course, be more overlap the closer species are to each other.) You may deeply and intellectually believe that this Quantitative/Discrete Realm (our alpha realm) is an illusion (for example, that it is "the Veil of Maya"), but if you wish to continue bodily functioning, you had better act as if it pictures reality. (Ramakrishna wrote that you cannot stay alive more than twenty-one days if you do not function in this realm.[2] I have no idea where he got that exact time limit, but I agree with him that there *is* a time limit!)

1. An entity is real if it has, at least in principle, consistent effects on other entities. If it does not have these effects, it is not real. If it is a singular event then different observers must all report the same observation for it to be real.

2. Algorithms are Markovian. Effect invariably follows cause without exception or variation. However, because of complexity, this often can only be perceived after the event. When it can be seen forward it is called "Natural Law." Free will is an illusion: all events are caused by preceding events. There are no exceptions.

3. The observables dealt with in this Realm are those to which the human sensory array responds directly or with the aid of mechanical or glass amplifiers.

4. Questions that can be answered in Realm i are How and Small What questions ("What is this?" "It is a chair."). Questions that cannot be answered in principle include Why and Large What questions ("What is the meaning of life?" "What happens when you die?"). *Moral questions cannot be answered in this Realm.* (Although we sometimes try with statements such as "Crime does not pay" or Plato's belief that a virtuous life led to a happier old age.) David Hume pointed out that from statements of fact you cannot develop statements of ought. And this is a Realm dealing primarily with perceived facts and entities inferred from them.[3]

5. Space is Newtonian, stretching infinitely in all directions,

everywhere the same. It is empty until filled with matter and is characterized by three basic attributes: continuity, infinity, uniformity. Time is also Newtonian, stretching forward and backward at the exact same rate with the razor edge of the present between. It goes on forever in both directions. Energy is defined as the ability to do work. A derrick controls more energy than a muscle since it can do more work.

6. The predominant geometry is Euclidean although in specific situations other geometries may be applied, i.e. to curved surfaces, to paths, and to shapes.

Realm ii - The Quantitative/Continuous Realm

This is the Realm in which entities and processes are quantitative and may be described numerically, but in which they are not discrete. All things flow into each other and are part of a dynamic gestalt in which a change in any part is a change in all parts. Relativity theory and field theory in general are part of this Realm.

1. In Realm ii, an entity is real if it is clearly conceived of, has consistent effects on other entities and has constants that can be numbered. Its *effect* on other entities must be consistent and must be observable. If another entity is conceptualized and has the same effects and is more elegant and/ or more fruitful, then the first is abandoned and no longer considered to be real.

2. Algorithms are Markovian. Free will is not an observable in this Realm.

3. Questions that can be answered are How questions and Small What questions, but not Why or Large What questions.

4. Space?
Time?
Energy?

5. Geometry is non-Euclidean.*

Realm iii - *The Non-quantitative/Discrete Realm*

This is the Realm in which events and entities are non-quantitative and are separate from each other. Oz comes quickly to mind. It is the Realm of the saga, the myth, the fairy tale. It is a Realm we frequently move into when common sense is not effective, when there is a strong need to attain a goal and there is no available technology to do this. In this Realm many entities and events cannot be quantified. In principle we cannot assign a number of miles or yards to the length of the Yellow Brick Road or assign numbers to the days and hours that Dorothy and her friends spent traversing it. Distances may be one, two, three, four, five, but after that they are pretty much short, long, very long. Entities

* It would be interesting to investigate the relationship between hodology (the mathematics of paths) and the geometry of Realm ii.

are numbered something like, "One, two, three, four, many, very many."

> 1. An entity is real to the degree that it is clearly conceived and/or has its existence acted upon. It is perfectly reasonable to say "Of course God is real. Look at the cathedral built to His glory." The spell which keeps the princess asleep in the woods is as real as the princess or the woods. The concept of experimental proof of the reality of an entity is irrelevant. Logical proof is also irrelevant.*
>
> The road to truth is inherent in the concept of the Realm itself. Unless you understand the dynamic and structure of the whole Realm, none of its parts make sense. Unless you understand everything, you do not understand anything.
>
> All important people are either all good or all bad; there are no in-betweens. If the wicked witch acts in a loving manner to children or flowers, we know that her love is not real, but a pretense. If the beautiful princess acts spitefully, we know her spitefulness is not real, but forced by a spell. As needed we invent new, clearly conceived and therefore real, entities to explain any non-coherent parts of the story. These include fate, destiny, karma and so forth. A world picture must be coherent and these are useful to keep it that way. *They are just as real as anything else.*
>
> In Realm iii, a verbal statement immediately and inex-

---

* For the Trobriand Islanders that Bruno Malinowski studied, "… the validity of a magical spell lay, not in its results, not in proof, but in its very being. To seek validity through proof was foreign to their thinking." (Dorothy Lee, "Codifications of Reality: Lineal and Non-lineal", *Psychosom Med,* March 1, 1950 12:89-97.)

orably *creates* its own referent. The clearer the statement, the more detailed is the referent. If I say "There is a ghost in the attic," then ghosts and attics are equally real, although there may or may not be a ghost upstairs at this moment. Both an entity in this Realm and symbols of it are equally real and interact. In this world picture part of an entity is equal to the whole and remains equal and interconnected, even if there is physical space and time between them. Burning the flag of a country *is* damaging to the country.

2. Algorithms are non-Markovian. Free will exists, but only within the limits of the pattern. The youngest prince cannot decide to stay permanently at home and not go on the quest. In a wartime world picture your enemy cannot decide to behave decently and honorably. If he seems to do this, it is a trick to gain some advantage. (See Chapter VI, page 121 for the effect of this on the Mideast conflict.)

3. Observables dealt with are those within the human sensory range and some beyond it.

4. Space is personal and is very different in different places. Generally space is centered around a protagonist and distances are near or far from this center. Space is not empty, but is filled with forces and energies. Time starts with an act of will and ends when the tensions created by this act are resolved. Time ends then, and they "live happily ever after" or have "the thousand-year Reich." The Hobbit cycle starts when the Ring itself wills to change its location.

"The Ring is on the move" and ends when the Ring is destroyed and the problems raised by its action are solved.

Energy is characteristic of all living beings and symbols of them (and some non-living entities), but is not evenly distributed. It is sometimes clearly defined and given such names as chi, mana, grey force, prana, wakenda, manitou and so forth. In the *Star Wars* sagas, people often express their good wishes for each other by saying, "May the Force be with you." Sometimes it is only implied, but it is the major factor in deciding outcomes. King Arthur had a great deal (some of which came to him with Excalibur) and was therefore invulnerable until treachery and betrayal redistributed the energy pattern.

5. Geometry is personal with distances measured not in quantitative units, but in the problems and obstacles between the main protagonist and his or her goals.

Realm iv - The Non-quantitative/Continuous Realm

This is the Realm in which all events and entities are non-quantitative and none is discrete. The universe is continuous and all events and entities flow into each other. The clearest example is our usual experience of our own mind and existence. In states of satori, cosmic consciousness, etc., both the cosmos and oneself are perceived as non-separate in this fashion. Logical thought does not exist in this Realm as there are no discrete entities. Language does not apply and perceptions are ineffable.

There is a particular belief widespread among certain quarters of the population both in the Western and the Eastern world, that a state of being exists, reached by a few — sometimes spontaneously and sometimes through hard work — that leaves a person different than he or she was before experiencing it. This state leaves the person much improved and with an insight into the true nature of reality, an insight very hard or impossible to put into words. The most usual English word for this state is enlightenment. In Zen it is called satori, in Yoga samadhi, in Sufism fana. Bucke called it cosmic consciousness, Gurdjieff objective consciousness, St. Paul "The peace of God that passes all understanding."

The people who believe that they have had this experience describe it very differently, but agree on certain aspects. The similarities appear to be as follows:

1. Everything in the universe is connected to everything else. This includes the self. The importance of anything lies in the fact that it is a part of everything else, not in its identity. The whole universe is perceived as "a one without a second." There is no separation between entities, neither by time nor by space. To everything in the universe one must and can legitimately say "Tat tvam asi," "That art thou."

2. There is a sense of rightness of all things in reality.

3. There is a knowing that this is the true and valid picture of reality.

4. There is a sense of having been profoundly changed.

5. There is an end to fear, including the fear of death.

6. A belief that the experience is ineffable — it cannot be described in words.

7. A belief that there is no substitute for the experience itself. One who has had it can only suggest to others how to work towards it and perhaps some of the mileposts on the path.

The experience cannot be conceptualized or described in ordinary language. Nor can the observables be translated into meaningful terms in other Realms. *The Cloud of Unknowing*, one of the great mystical documents of the Medieval period, states one Realm iv observable: "Of God Himself can no man think. He may well be loved, but not thought. By love He may be gotten and holden. By thought, never."

St. Catherine of Siena wrote: "All that can be said of God is not God."

All agree that there is a knowledge that there are no separation lines in reality. Some call this all-inclusive One God. Some do not. Some see God as a part of the One. Some do not. This choice appears to depend on where you started from. Afterwards some go on doing the same things that they did before the experience but with a very different attitude. Some change their way of life. Some try to help others to achieve the experience, some do not.

However, the universal aspects, those that all seem to agree on, do not appear to depend on where you started from, but from the structure and dynamics of the experience — the state of being — itself.

A few typical statements illustrate these points:

"I was suddenly immersed in Itness. I did not call it by that name. I had no need for words. It and I were one." — Bernard Berenson

"All is God and there is no God." — Rinpoche

"God is a stone in a stone, a straw in a straw, and an angel in an angel." — John Donne

"They reckon ill who leave me out. When me they fly, I am the wings. I am the doubter and the doubt. I am the hymn the Brahman sings." — Emerson

"Before Enlightenment I chopped wood and carried water. After Enlightenment I chopped wood and carried water." — Zen saying

One statement of this is the Buddhist "Nirvana." In this concept a person becomes so completely a part of the One in which there is neither time nor space that the person "is freed from the wheel of things" as there are no happenings or events in a cosmos in what is, was and will be.

From the viewpoint of this book, satori seems to be a deep immersion in a Realm iv world picture. Realm iv is a closed gestalt, a world picture in which there is no *pregnanz*, no tension towards completion. In this way it fundamentally differs from experience in other Realms. Perhaps partially because of this, a deep experience of Realm iv often seems to produce a very strong psychological effect and sometimes leads the person involved to the belief (apparently for some a valid belief) that he or she has been permanently changed in a positive direction.

The idea that one achieves perfection through the experience is an Eastern concept that rarely survives the thinking processes (contact with the general world picture) of the Western world. Here many tend rather to believe that there was, at best, only one being in all history who approached the level of perfection and He wound up on a Cross at Golgotha.

This being said, it is also true that many of the people who claimed to have had this experience represent the finest of our race and that their behavior afterwards often seems to bear out the claims made.

In summary:

1. All entities and processes conceived and perceived are real. The road to truth is being a part of the whole. Perception and feeling are not separate.

2. Algorithms are non-Markovian. The cosmos and perceiver

flow harmoniously but unpredictably. Since there is no separation, free will is not a category.

3. Questions cannot be asked, but Why and Large What questions are often answered to the satisfaction of the individual.

4. Space and time are not relevant concepts.

5. Geometry is not a relevant concept.

ǝ̂yp

It is important to be aware that none of these Realms rests on solid, absolute and unquestionable grounds. Since they are human inventions, they stand on foundations which are shaky as soon as one looks closely at them. (For example, in Realm i there are entities which remain stable over time, entities such as rocks. This, of course, is illusory and the apparent stability is only due to our limited senses as we do not perceive the constant movement and change of the microparticles of which they are built.) All taxonomies with the possible exception of geometry have this problem, although even there one might remark that the entities defined as observables in plane geometry rest on the concept of an absolutely flat surface. An example of this is, to put it mildly, difficult to find. The value of a classification system rests not in its logical structure, but in its usefulness. One proves a pudding by eating it and the usefulness of this classification system will have to be tried by appropriate tests.

So far in this book I have only dealt with a very broad level of the classification system of world pictures. This primary grouping of world pictures is, in itself, of value and brings new insights into many difficult problems. It is, however, a far cry from Linnaeus' ladder of groupings from Kingdom to Species.

Further development of the present taxonomy, beyond the Realm level, will have to be left to the future. However, one example of how this may develop can be shown here.

Realm iii is the Realm in which the observables are discrete and non-quantitative. For Realm iii, the next level is A, the Realm of Magic and B, the Realm of Non-magic. In A, the Realm of Magic, the two laws of magic — the law of similarity and the law of contagion — are valid. In B, they are not valid.

The law of similarity is that if two observables have similar characteristics, they have similar effects. Thus if a plant has leaves that resemble a healthy heart, the plant will be a good medicine for a damaged heart. In all rain-making ceremonies I sprinkle water on the ground, actually or symbolically, so that it will rain.

The law of contagion states that once two observables have been in contact they remain in contact and are part of a larger whole forever. Your cut and discarded fingernails are still and forever a part of you and if (combining both laws) I make a model or doll that somewhat resembles you and put the discarded fingernails on the hand, then whatever I do to the doll (cut, burn, stab, for example) will be felt by you without regard to the space between you and the model. If I have been born on a certain date, then that date will affect me all the rest of my life.

These two laws somehow seem valid to us when we observe their functioning. (Astrology is very widely accepted in human history.) They feel right because we are so familiar with them. They are basic to the way that the human unconscious operates and to the laws of association of our own mental functioning. (When the psychologists of the first half of the 20th century did their extensive research into how we associate different things and how we remember these associations, these two laws were major factors in their findings.)

It is interesting perhaps to note here that magic (actions or thoughts in iii-A) has only psychological effects and does not affect physical observables (observables in Realm i) directly. Thus the magical practice of voodoo only brings psychological results. It has no effect unless the person who is hexed knows that the hexing has taken place. He may then die of it, but we are dealing with hysterical or psychosomatic causes.

The second group of world pictures in B of Realm iii is the group which follows the basic limiting principles of this realm, but in which the laws of magic do not operate. We see this in the typical saga or fairy tale. In Oz the Ruby Slippers are not evil because they were worn by a wicked witch. They are what they are. In Oz the basic limiting principles of Realm iii are followed but not the laws of magic.

Each of these can (and hopefully will) be analyzed further. The trunk of the taxonomic tree is all World Pictures. The first four main branches are Realms i, ii, iii and iv. Each of these Realms divides into domains, and as many categories as is needed. This analysis proceeds as long as it is fruitful — as long as it produces useful results.

✃

A final thought about these definitions seems worth emphasizing before proceeding further.

It appears advisable to recapitulate here a point that is very hard for us as 20th and 21st century Westerners to accept. It is an aspect of this work that can easily be overlooked. This is that the term "existence" has a very different meaning in each of the four Realms. From the viewpoint of *Landscapes of the Mind*, an entity exists if and only if:

In Realm i.   *The Quantitative/Discrete Realm*

It has consistent and (theoretically at least) mathematically describable effects on other entities.

In Realm ii.   *The Quantitative/Continuous Realm*

It is the most elegant construct that can be found to account for the data and has constants that can be measured and dealt with mathematically. Gravity is an example.

In Realm iii.   ***The Non-quantitative/Discrete Realm***
It is clearly conceived and/or acted upon.

In Realm iv.   ***The Non-quantitative/Continuous Realm***
It is perceived as an integral part of the All, the One that includes everything that exists and in which nothing can be quantified and from which nothing can be separated.

V.
Some Implications of the Classification System: Technology and World Pictures

The difficulty we feel about consciousness is not a
local one that can be resolved by relating it directly
to physics. It is one of relating our whole inner and
outer viewpoints — of finding a context in which
the subjective and objective aspects of life can be
intelligibly connected.
— *Mary Midgley*

The aim of the true voyage of discovery is
to seek not new vistas but new eyes.
— *Marcel Proust*

Technology and Myth

The taxonomy of four basic Realms of Experience will
need much further development than this introductory
book can provide. Yet in its present form it allows us to
illuminate a number of subjects.

When we have the technology to act so as to produce
the results we want on at least a fairly consistent basis
we generally use Realm i — the Quantitative/Discrete

Realm. We act rationally according to the technology. We put out a campfire with water, not with spells and chants. When we do not have the technology to achieve this level of results we frequently shift to Realm iii — the Non-quantitative/Discrete Realm. Knowing I will have to fly through the anti-aircraft fire at a certain height and having no way (no technology) to predict whether or not it will hit me, I make sure I am wearing my lucky socks and carrying my rabbit's foot charm. ("To us the most essential point about magic and religion is that it only steps in where knowledge has failed." B. Malinowski.[1]) When I am filling the plane's gas tank and securely tightening the gas cap, I am not concerned with amulets and charms. As Malinowski further has pointed out, Trobriand Islanders who intend to go fishing in the known waters of the lagoon do not add charms and spells to their preparations. When they are going to fish in less known waters they do add them.*

★ Many others have pointed out that it is important to know in what Realm your immediate problem and goals are, and to function as clearly and completely as possible in that Realm.

> since feeling is first
> who pays any attention
> to the syntax of things
> will never wholly kiss you;
>
> wholly to be a fool
> while spring is in the world.
>
> (e.e. cummings, *100 Selected Poems*, New York, Grove Press, undated, p. 35.)

It is not only in war and peace in kingdoms with and without technology that we use these two different pictures of reality, these two different *Weltbilds*. Ernst Cassirer pointed out that we generally use one when we are dealing with technical problems such as designing a better automobile engine and the other when we are dealing with problems in human relationships and political action.

> If we look at the present state of our cultural life we feel at once that there is a deep chasm between two different fields. When it comes to political action man seems to follow rules quite different from those recognized in all his mere theoretical activities. No one would think of solving a problem of natural science or a technical problem by the methods that are recommended and put into action in the solution of political questions. In the first case we never aim to use anything but rational methods. Rational thought holds its ground here and seems constantly to enlarge its field. Scientific knowledge and technical mastery of nature daily win new and unprecedented victories. But in man's practical and social life the defeat of rational thought seems to be complete and irrevocable. In this domain modern man is supposed to forget everything he has learned in the development of his intellectual life. He is admonished to go back to the first rudimentary stages of human culture. Here rational and scientific thought openly confess their breakdown; they surrender to their most dangerous enemy.[2]

The different Realms of the world pictures vary so much in their basic assumptions about many aspects of reality that they will often lead to very different solutions to a problem. Sometimes these conclusions will be directly opposite to each other and yet each be completely logical and valid in terms of the world picture in which it was drawn.

A case in point is the decision to bomb an enemy civilian population in wartime when you have control of the air. The results of this in terms of the morale of the bombed population are clear. In the World War II Blitz when the Germans intensively bombed London, the bombing *raised* the morale and determination of the British population to fight. When the Allies gained air superiority they then bombed the German cities. In spite of very heavy bombing this in no way lowered the German morale, and by 1944-45 when city after city had been terribly damaged German war production was at its highest level. The extensive American bombing of North Vietnam raised the morale and determination of the North Vietnamese to win. Whatever is going on here?

From the classification system viewpoint the situation is as follows. The decision to commence and continue the bombing is made by planners who are using a sensory world picture: Realm i, the Quantitative/Discrete Realm. In this Western common-sense *Weltbild*, world picture, it is only reasonable and is a coldly logical conclusion that if your cities are being bombed and there is little that your country can do about it, and the enemy keeps showing that they can do as they wish to any part of your country, and you see the destruction increasing every day, it is a clear sign that you are losing the war and that continuing it will only increase the pain and loss. That your morale will, under these conditions be lowered and that you will be more and more inclined to surrender is an obvious conclusion. So obvious a truth is it that you will have a very strong psychological tendency to ignore or forget previous examples to the contrary and go right on with the bombing as the best way to win the war.

However, the people who are being bombed generally move into a different, a mythic world picture: Realm iii, the Non-quantitative/Discrete Realm, and here the conclusions to the perceived situation are very different. If you are part of a population that is being bombed at the will of the enemy and there is nothing you can do about it except try to be in a shelter which may or may not survive a direct hit and to which, in any case, you cannot take your home and possessions, you are at the mercy of unpredictable disasters and do not have the *technology* to predict or avoid them in any reliable manner. In problematic situations of this sort, human beings generally shift from their sensory world picture (Realm i) to a mythic world construction (Realm iii). This is the world of the saga and fairy tale and in it the good guys *always* win at the end. By definition we are the good guys. The road to victory is often long and hard, the prince may have terrible and painful obstacles to overcome on his quest, but each of these is not a sign of weakness, it is a sign of *progress towards an eventual victory* if only the faith is kept. "Conquer we must for our cause it is just" goes the old song and who in a war believes they are fighting on the unjust side?[3]

Further, each bombing strengthens the belief that "they" are the bad ones with whom it is impossible to negotiate because "they" always lie while "we" tell the truth. If the enemy is all bad then surrender becomes more and more impossible and it is, in spite of our ruined streets and reduced rations, more and more certain that we will eventually win.

In the mythic world picture there very often is a quest (ranging from a search for *Lebensraum* to Frodo bringing the ring to Mount Doom to carrying a basket to grand-mother's house to bringing back an errant wife from Troy), terrible problems on the quest, and surmounting them to living happily ever after.

Since neither side understands that the other is making emotional and action decisions in a different world picture, the bombing continues and accomplishes the opposite of its planned goal and the cost in children and adults blasted and incinerated continues to rise.

Inter-realm Communication

One aspect of consciousness which is very little understood at present concerns the fact that we seem to mostly use a mix of world pictures at any one time and rarely a pure case of only one.

Most human situations contain a mixture of areas in which we have the technology we need to achieve consistent results and areas in which we do not. We effortlessly slip back and forth from one world picture to another and in our resultant behavior. I may be going to church to pray for good health the following year, but I look at the traffic lights on the way there and cross on the green and not the red. A *Weltbild*, a world picture, is usually defined more by the areas in which we do not have a reliable technology than by the areas in which we do. I define a world picture by the fact that I am praying (a Realm iii activity), not by the fact that, at the same time, I put my prayer book down on the table so it will not fall to the ground (a Realm i activity).

Another example of how we slip easily between Realms is the contrast in Chapter I (page 25) showing the differences in the perception of reality generally held by the population of a country at peace and by the same population when they are enthusiastically involved in a war. What is shown regarding the wartime world picture is valid, though it is usually only applied to certain aspects of reality.

One aspect of the wartime construction of reality is the fact that it is usually applied to only two general areas: (1) human behavior and interaction; (2) the great forces of the cosmos. It is not applied to things, to tools, implements, or other articles of everyday life, where we have the requisite technology to solve our problems. The most dedicated communists, the most fanatical Nazis, the most extreme religious fundamentalists all know that if they want certain types of food to be edible, the food must be cooked; that if those foods are left on the fire too long they will be burned; and so forth. In such dealings, they know that a peacetime construction of reality (Realm i) holds true. We may regard the enemy as the great Satan and firmly believe that after he is defeated we will all live happily ever after (Realm iii, the mythic Realm), but we know that in order to wage war we must buy weapons, have cartridges that fit our rifles, and teach our gunners Euclidean geometry so they can hit their targets (Realm i, the sensory Realm). We are perfectly clear about how these two methods of construing reality relate to each other, and about when and where to use each. We may be going to a great crusade in God's name to make the world safe for democracy, but we drive on the correct side of the street to get there. "All my means are sane, my object and motives are mad," said Captain Ahab of his great mythic (Realm iii) quest for Moby Dick.

We live usually in the two Realms reciprocally. As one increases, the other diminishes. As we gain technology (including the method of gaining more knowledge and therefore increasing the area in which we can get reliable results from our actions) the second part decreases. Alchemy gives way to chemistry.

The reverse can also happen. We are fighting a war which we confidently expect to win because we have faith in our superior arms. The military situation changes and the enemy now seems as likely to win as we are. Our predictability has changed. After Stalingrad and the loss of the Africa Corps, Hitler's attitude toward the war became much more mythical than it had been prior to those events.

This differentiation between the two parts of a world picture — and some of its implications — has been known for a long time. In the 5th century B.C., Plato wrote in the *Euthyphro*:

Socrates: And what sort of differences creates enmity and anger? Suppose for example that you and I, my good friend, differ about a number; do differences of this sort make us enemies and set us at variance with one another? Do we not go at once to arithmetic, and put an end to them by a sum?

Euthyphro: True.

Socrates: Or suppose that we differ about magnitude, do we not quickly end the difference by measuring?

Euthyphro: Very true.

Socrates: And we end a controversy about heavy and light by resorting to a measuring machine?

Euthyphro: To be sure.

Socrates: But what differences are there which cannot be thus decided and which therefore make us angry and set us at enmity with one another? I dare say the answer does not occur to you at the moment and therefore I will suggest that these enmities arise when the matters of difference are the just and unjust, good and evil, honorable and dishonorable, etc. Are not these the points about which men differ, and about which when we are unable satisfactorily to decide our differences, you and I and all of us quarrel, when we do quarrel? (Jowett translation)

The situation of consciousness thus is made more complex by the fact that most situations contain two reciprocal parts. In one of them we have the technology to achieve reliable results from our actions. In the other, we do not. The percentage of each varies with the particular combination of our perception of what is going on and our own needs. We all agree on the first part — at least in those areas where we share technology. Nearly all humans, regardless of their culture, agree that a fire can be put out with water. Except in very special cases (such as a fire declared "holy" or "an everlasting flame") we do not accompany our water dumping with spells, magic or use a field theory approach. We rely simply, all of us, on our practical knowledge — our technology. If we want a stone to fly farther, we throw it harder and generalize this easily to baseballs, javelins and fish hooks. The first part then is the one we believe all sane people, if they have the technology, would agree on.

> If someone maintains that two and two are five, or that
> Iceland is on the equator, you feel pity rather than anger....
> The most savage controversies are those about matters as to
> which there is no good evidence either way. Persecution is
> used in theology, not in arithmetic....
>
> — Bertrand Russell[4]

The other part of each life-situation concerns areas in which we do *not* have the technology to achieve reliable results from our behavior — areas in which we do not regularly get positive feedback when we act. We might loosely divide this second part of each situation (the part in which we shift to a mythic [Realm iii] viewpoint) into three aspects.

1. Problematic situations: Fishing in unknown waters for a Trobriand Island native. An American in a sailboat who is becalmed. An automobile breaking down with a driver who knows nothing about motors. These, and many others, are situations where one is dealing with objects and things, but simply does not have the information to know how to act so as to attain one's goals or the method of finding out this information.

2. The nature of other human beings: We have many rules of thumb for dealing with other persons, but no way of attaining general rules that will insure a reliable response.

To predict exactly how another person will act in a specific situation is beyond us.

3. General metaphysics: How the cosmos is run. The existence (and definition) of God. What is death. There is no reliable technology for affecting the universe no matter how deeply we feel our intercessory prayer.

I may be in a world picture in which I am going at the behest of God to build a temple on a mountain, or to do volunteer work for Habitat for Humanity or to donate blood to the Red Cross or to bomb an abortion clinic, but to get there I drive on the right side of the road if I am in the United States and on the left side if I am in England, and make sure that my car has gasoline in the tank in both countries. And I simply do not notice how completely and easily I have made major changes in the way I organize my sensory input into a coherent whole.

VI.
Dealing with the World Pictures of Terrorists:
The Problem of Fundamentalism

There is nothing so helpless as reason
when faced with unreason.
— *Santayana*

There is, at the beginning of the 21ˢᵗ century, a rising tide of fundamentalism all over the world. Put another way, there is an increasing tendency among larger and larger population groups to use a Realm iii approach to solving social and political problems. There is, in this system, one way of arriving at truth ("*Our* scripture"), the world is divided into good and bad people, the conflict is basic and its outcome will determine the future. In short, a switch from peacetime view to wartime view.

When we are not constantly reinforced in our belief about how-the-world-is-and-works, when new views are thrust upon us by the recently arrived presence of radio and television constantly telling us how other groups than our own see the world, when everything seems to be changing and nothing seems solid and everlasting, then it is very tempting to find a simpler way to organize reality. We begin to see one faith and metaphysics as the *right* way, the only way, and all others as evil. When we do this, all our problems appear to be solved. We have an answer to everything and there are no more upsetting complications.

A clear example of this is given by Arthur Koestler when he described his conversion to a fundamentalist organization of reality, in this case to Communism.

> I was already reaping the reward of all conversions, a bliss-fully clear conscience…something had clicked in my brain which shook me like a mental explosion. To say that one had "seen the light" is a poor description of the mental rap-ture which only the convert knows (regardless of the faith he has been converted to). The new light seems to pour from all directions across the skull; the whole universe falls into a pattern like the stray pieces of a jigsaw puzzle as-sembled by magic at one stroke. There is now an answer to every question, doubts, conflicts are a matter of the tortured past — a past already remote, when one had lived in dismal ignorance of the tasteless, colorless world of those who *don't know*. Nothing henceforward can disturb the convert's inner peace and serenity — except the occasional fear of losing faith….[1]

Max Wertheimer, one of the first psychologists to insist that human beings organize their worldview in a coherent and comprehensible way, wrote of this tenden-cy when under stress for us to shift from that Realm i world picture to a Realm iii construction of reality. He wrote of:

> ...the almost irresistible tendency, the strong desire to get a simple decisive structuralization of the field...to get clear orientation...without the features of "because," "but," "nevertheless," "although," and so forth. Men are unhappy if the complication of such factors befogs the issue.[2]

We see here one reason for the drive to fundamentalism. Fundamentalism presents a much easier to live with world picture than the liberal position. Everything is clear with one guiding source and principle. The organization of the world is simple and straightforward. This is one reason why it is so much easier to get into a war than it is to get out of one.

That there is this human tendency to a terrible and fateful simplicity in the ways we organize reality does not mean that it cannot be overcome. In all modern wars where the overwhelming mass of the population has opted for a Realm iii, wartime world picture, there have been a percentage of individuals who stood strongly against it and held onto the less "good gestalt" quality of the Realm i liberal position. As we clarify this with the aid of the taxonomy, we can learn to deal with it more effectively. As the philosopher Hegel pointed out, the more understanding we have of a limitation the closer we are to being free of it.

At the beginning of the 21st century the United

States is facing a new type of conflict. This is the highly organized and effective action of terrorists against a major country in the form of sabotage, murder and biowarfare. The threat of chemical and even nuclear attack is in the air.

The terrorists have, by their statements and actions, made clear the world picture which they are primarily using. It is what I have earlier described (page 104) as the world construction used by people emotionally involved in a war (Realm iii). With what has been learned in this exploration so far, it may be worthwhile to look at this description again.

In Peacetime	*In Wartime*
Realm i.	Realm iii.
	(The terrorist's world construction.)
1. Good and Evil have many shades of grey. Many opinions and groups with different ideas are legitimate. Things and opinions are seen as relatively good and bad, satisfactory or unsatisfactory, stupid or intelligent.	Good and Evil are "We" and "They." There are no innocent bystanders; you are for us or against us. The crucial parts of the world are divided into black and white. Opinions on this are absolutely right or wrong.

2. "Now" is pretty much like other times. There are more of some things, less of others, but the differences are quantitative.

"Now" is special, qualitatively different from all other times. Everything is cast in the balance; who wins now wins forever. It is the time of the final battle between good and evil, of Armageddon, of Ragnarok, of the War to End Wars. "It is the final battle," says the Internationale.

3. The great forces of nature, such as God or human evolution, are not particularly involved in our disputes.

"God Wills It," "*Dieu et mon droit*," "History fights on our side," "Manifest Destiny," and other such slogans indicate our belief that the great forces of the cosmos are for "Us" and against "Them".

4. When this present period is over, things will go on pretty much as they have in the past.

When this war is over, everything will be vastly different. If we win, much better; if we lose, terribly worse. The world will be deeply changed by what we do here. Winning or losing will change the meaning of the past and the shape of the future.

5. There are many problems to be solved and their relative importance varies from day to day. Life is essentially complex with many foci.

There is only one major problem to be solved. All others are secondary. Life is essentially simple. It has one major focus.

6. All people act from pretty much the same motives.

"They" act from a wish for power. "We" act from self-defense, benevolence, and reasons of common decency and morality. Everyone is either for us or against us. There are no neutrals.

7. Problems start on many levels, e.g., economic, political, personal, and must be dealt with on these levels.

The real problem started with an act of will on the part of the enemy and can only be solved by breaking his will or by making him helpless to act on it.

8. We are concerned with the causes of problems we are trying to solve.

We are not concerned with causes, only with outcomes.

9. We can talk with those with whom we disagree. Negotiation is possible.

Since the enemy is evil, he naturally lies. Communication is not possible.

10. All people are fundamentally the same. Differences are quantitative.

"We" and "They" are qualitatively different, so different that the same actions are "good" when we do them, "evil" when the enemy does them. There is doubt that they and we really belong to the

The wartime world picture is in Realm iii, the Realm of saga and myth, the Non-quantitative/Discrete Realm. The peacetime world picture is in Realm i, the world as perceived by the human sensory array, the Quantitative/Discrete Realm.

If I am a part of one Realm and in a conflict or dispute with someone who is a part of another, and if I am not clearly aware of this, then many of my actions will not have the effect I expect. I have tried earlier to demonstrate this with the discussion of the futility of bombing the enemy infrastructure when you have control of the air — an action which usually tends to strengthen the enemy's resolve and increase his morale. You generally get the opposite of the effect which you are trying to produce.

There is at this moment in history (2011) an intelligent, well-intentioned group in the United States which believes that we should stop all offensive military action and tell our opponents — Iran, the Taliban and al-Qaeda — that we understand their frustration and how it led to their actions, and we forgive them and that we should all sit down like civilized adults and listen to each other, and talk the matter through and come to a peaceful solution. This is an excellent and reasonable suggestion from a Realm i viewpoint, from the Realm which produced it. However, the terrorists are perceiving a world picture in a Realm iii Domain. In this world construction an enemy is *all* bad, has absolutely no redeeming features and *never tells the truth*. Any such offer would be regarded inevitably either as a trick to gain some advantage or an admission of weakness which should logically be reacted to by more and stronger attacks.

In a situation where your enemy is using a Realm iii approach, where he sees the conflict as between absolute evil and absolute good and one being fought for the future as well as the present, you cannot deal reasonably with him from a Realm i viewpoint because he logically *cannot* believe that you have any good intentions.

The way to deal with the situation is to retain your own Realm i orientation but be clearly aware that your conflict is with a person or group that has a world picture in which *you* are the hopelessly evil, unredeemable, always-lying dragon and he is St. George. This may limit your options, but at least whichever one you choose will have predictable results.

In 1990, in a desperate attempt to end the Mideast bloodbath, the then Israeli Prime Minister, Ehud Barak, made a startling offer to the Palestinians. Barak was in an unusual position to make the offer — he had been the most decorated soldier in the Israeli Army and his loyalty, dedication and experience were unquestionable. He offered nearly everything that the Palestinians had been demanding — 90 percent of the West Bank, East Jerusalem, control of part of the Temple Mount, etc. The Israeli public was shocked at the size of the offer (In the words of one Israeli newspaper, "He gave away the store"), but generally were ready to accept it if the Palestinians would do their part and stop the attacks on civilians, the bombs in buses and the suicide bombers in supermarkets.

This unexpected offer, far more than anything that had previously been put on the table, was expected to provoke, at the very least, a counteroffer and negotiations and to be a large and real step toward peace. What *did* happen was unpredictable from a common sense (Realm i) viewpoint and completely predictable from the concept of world pictures and their relationship to consciousness.

The Israelis were using a world picture in a Domain in Realm i. In this Quantitative/Discrete, Western common sense Realm (read "Kansas" or see the description of the general peacetime world picture in Chapter I), this offer would be seen as what it was — at worst a point for further negotiations, at best a major attempt to end the bloodbath and to convince the Palestinians that the Israelis were serious in their search for peace. It was by far the most generous offer that had ever been made in the long negotiations and should, from the viewpoint of

Realm i, have advanced the peace process by a long and crucial step.

However, the Arabs were using a world picture in a Domain of Realm iii (read "Oz," or see the description of the general wartime world picture). In accord with the basic limiting principles of this Non-quantitative/ Discrete Realm, they logically made no counteroffer, raised new and clearly impossible-to-accept conditions for peace, broke off negotiations and immediately increased the violence — the *Intifada*.

In Realm iii everything tends to be black or white; there are often no shades of grey. The enemy is implacably evil, *always* lies and, to the point here, would *never* give up an advantage or concede a negotiating point unless either it had to because of weakness or it was some sort of trick to gain a new advantage. These two are, from the viewpoint of Realm iii the only possible reasons such an offer would be made. Using the basic limiting principles of this Realm it would have been completely illogical for the Palestinians to accept the offer or to conceive that it was made in good faith.

Not seeing how it could be a trick, they had to assume that it was made through weakness. It seemed obvious and clear to them that the Israelis had been so devastated and weakened by their suicide bombing policy that if they increased it they could get even more than had been offered, perhaps even attain their ideal goal of the total collapse and destruction of the State of Israel.

Neither side understood that their opponent had defined the-way-the-world-works far differently than they had themselves. Both behaved logically and reasonably from their own viewpoint. Real communication and mutual understanding was impossible. If there had been understanding of this difference on either side, a quite different set of options would have been seen as both possible and necessary.

If the approach presented by this book seems to limit the usual ways we have to solve problems such as how to deal with the terrorism, it also leads to new possibilities, to new methods. As an example of how we might use the viewpoint of this book, I will take the problem of the general animosity that is now building up between the Middle Eastern Mohammedan world and the Western European and American world. As shown by the example of the Barak-Palestinian disaster, a large part of the problem is that one group was primarily using a Realm i (sensory) world picture and the other a Realm iii (mythic) one. It is very difficult, if not impossible, to convince people using a Realm iii approach to change it to a Realm i world picture. Logic and reason are frustratingly ineffectual. However, the group using a sensory (Kansas) world picture can *understand* the mythic (Oz) world picture of the other group and work effectually within it. For our purposes here, a mythic approach usually includes:

1. A division of all people into good and bad, both at the extreme and clearly defined. (There is no problem of who

is who in *Cinderella*.)

2. A great quest by the good guys to solve a very important problem:

The quest has:

   A. A great goal which emotionally involves us.

   B. A practical way of reaching the goal, fraught with great difficulties.

   C. A "happily-ever-after" end point.

Working within this viewpoint the task becomes to redefine the quest so that it includes both groups as good guys. Imagine, for example, a leading statesman of either group in conflict today making this major speech (an inaugural address or at the UN).

We, in the East and in the West, have major problems with each other. They must and will be solved before we can have real peace. But while we struggle and seek for solutions, children are starving to death all over the world. This is not permissible. The terribly hungry children must come first. Whatever our goal and God, whatever terrible political and personal injustices that have been done to us, we *must* first make certain that no child in the world is crying helplessly and in pain as he or she dies of starvation. Everything else

can wait. What can we, you and I and all of us, all human beings, do about this? We personally will immediately allocate
at least as much money as we now spend on weapons to
see that no child in the world dies of hunger. But we cannot do this alone. We can only succeed together. These are
our human children who are suffering and dying. They are
not black or white, yellow or brown, Moslem or Christian,
Hindu or Buddhist, or divided in any other way. They are
our children. They must come first.

The speaker has redefined the problem in a practical,
mythic, Realm iii way that makes it possible for both
groups to join in and very difficult for either to refuse. In
the deepest sense, he has met his opponents where they
are and spoken to them in their own language.

In the mythic world picture you do not tell the young
prince not to go on a quest or try to reason him out of
it. Doing so will get you nowhere. You enlist him in a
greater quest. In the saga it would have been hopeless to
try to convince Eric the Red not to go to Greenland.
But he could have been convinced to go on to America.
Or the Prince to take Cinderella and together go off to
found a great new kingdom where peace and happiness
for all would exist forever. Instead of an "us" and "them"
he (or she) has stated the situation so as to build a "we."

If you are in conflict with someone and are using
different world pictures, you cannot solve the problem
by the methods appropriate to yours. You must see the
world he lives in with *his* eyes (walk a mile in his moc-

casins) and solve it with an appropriate method. This leads to new opportunities to solve apparently intractable problems.

After the problem is solved there are always others, "Medical care for all older people" or "all children" or "Save the planet," etc. New attitudes are thus built up. After you have fought in the wars for England long enough, it is hard to keep considering yourself primarily a Welshman or a Cornishman rather than an Englishman.

The goal should be clearly defined. Only one at a time. (The prince, in the fairy tale, goes on a quest for a single goal. Dorothy only wants to go home to Kansas.) The problem must be too great for any person or country to solve individually and too pressing to be delayed. It must be one that, almost no matter our metaphysical system, the great forces of the cosmos would approve. This solution has, of course, been suggested before. However, it grows naturally out of the taxonomy which also makes clear its potential value. Other possible solutions to seemingly intractable problems are also suggested by this approach.

VII.
World Pictures and the Structure of Consciousness

Three baseball umpires were arguing as to
what was a strike and what was a ball.
The first said, "I calls them as they are."
The second said, "I calls them as I see them."
The third said, "Until I calls them they ain't nothing."

Let us start by looking a little further into the problem
of communication between a person using one world
picture and a person using another. We will begin our
exploration with the general world picture used in the
film *Casablanca*. Much of the film occurs in Rick's Café,
a nightclub in Casablanca during World War II. The
general world picture of the movie was a Domain in
Realm i, the Realm of Quantitative/Discrete entities
and processes. If, in *Casablanca* a soldier from the Realm
i film *All Quiet on the Western Front* (say, Lew Ayres
playing Paul Baumer) came in the front door of Rick's
Café, we would manage to deal with the interruption
in one way or another. We might explain it on the
basis of a crazy person, demented by the stress of the

times, or by someone trying to reawaken memories in others of the past glories of France or in other ways. It could be a dream of the World War I soldier, or a flash to something happening later in life. It would be possible to continue the plot of the original film or even that of *All Quiet*. In any event, we would be confused, but not disoriented, startled but not threatened by the event. We could maintain a coherent view of either film. But if, when the door opened, it revealed Dorothy, Toto, the Scarecrow, the Tin Woodman and the Cowardly Lion, we could not maintain both the Realm i world picture of *Casablanca* and the Realm iii world picture of *The Wizard of Oz*. The intruders clearly come from a different Realm of world pictures than that of Rick's Café. One or the other has to give up and collapse. Either Dorothy and her friends are considered to be revelers on their drunken way to a masquerade, or all of the nightclub, its walls and characters, are illusions made up by the Wicked Witch in order to trap Dorothy and her team. The two world pictures are too different, are from different Realms and *cannot* be reconciled without the complete collapse of one or both of them. Either Dorothy or Rick can be real, but not both in the same scene.

This seems a farfetched example and not too helpful in our quest. However, suppose we try to generalize what we have learned. What happens when a well-meaning, liberal and a fundamentalist (or a physicist and an astrologer) try to communicate? The general world pictures which they are using come from two different Realms. Both are faced with the threat of overwhelming anxiety if they really *hear* the other. Each has a consciousness built on one world picture and a collapse of that world picture is perceived as a threatened collapse of the ego. The reaction to this is so terrifying that its technical name is "catastrophic anxiety." It is not a matter of changing minor aspects (such as which war was portrayed in the first two films mentioned above). The two films, one showing Rick and the other showing Paul Baumer, use the same general world picture and information can be exchanged between them and communication established. Dorothy and Rick come from films using world pictures in different Realms and there can be no meaningful information exchange between them without the complete collapse of one world picture, the other, or both. The liberal and the fundamentalist are in a similar situation and each will resist as strongly as possible accepting the other's viewpoint as valid. The threat of the collapse of one's general world picture is terrifying on deep human levels and the very possibility of it raises catastrophic anxiety. We resist this threat with all our power. Only special techniques and extraordinary situations can enable the gap to be bridged. And we know very little about the special techniques and situations needed to accomplish this. Sometimes, overwhelming physical stimuli, such as the collapse in 1945 Germany of the Nazi viewpoint under a complete breakdown of services and supplies and the inexorable advance from

West and East of the Allied Armies, seem to be effective. The heavy pressure of deprogramming techniques worked out by those who specialize in rescuing adolescents from cults often works, as does A.A. with alcoholics. Drugs and other organic techniques affecting the brain may have such an effect. Although we know so little about these techniques and situations at the present, recognizing the structure of the problem may be helpful in advancing our understanding.

The Structure of Consciousness

Very possibly the single most important insight which has emerged from this work so far is that the form and dynamic of the structure and flow of consciousness at any moment is an *adaptation* to a perceived relationship.

A relationship is perceived between the needs of the individual and the environmental situation. This perception results in a world picture, a *Weltbild*, a design of how-the-world-is-and-works, being chosen. This seems to be an immediate and automatic choice of the most elegant and useful world picture of all those available to the person. *It includes a set of rules for action to solve the problems involved in this relationship.*

As this is chosen, consciousness automatically adapts itself to the world design and conforms to the structure and dynamic of the design. Consciousness thus is a mirror image of the world picture. The structure and dynamics of "Inscape" and "Landscape" reflect each other. They are isomorphic. Which comes first is a chicken or egg type of question and has no meaning.

There can be no statements about the "true and defini-
tive structure of consciousness" because consciousness has no
permanent structure. It has no stable and describable form.
Consciousness takes on and has the same structure and
dynamics as the world picture which is being perceived and
reacted to at that moment. We can say, "This is the struc-
ture of consciousness at this particular moment." We cannot
say, "This is the structure of consciousness."

We are coldly logical and completely concerned only
with the future effects of our actions while seated at a
chessboard. In another situation we are wildly erotic and
the relationship between the body of our beloved and
our tension fills and organizes all our consciousness. Or,
consumed by rage at another time we may have no concern at all about the effect of our actions beyond the next
moment. *Consciousness is very different in each of these cases*
and, in each case, its form and dynamic is an adaptation
to the perceived relationship between our needs and the
perceived environment.

There is a definition implied here of a "human being" as an organism that chooses a Realm of Experience, defines it as real and acts, and reacts in terms of this
choice. An "animal" from this viewpoint is restricted
in its perceptions to one Realm only, but may shift the
Domain to which it is reacting to other Domains within
the same Realm.

This seems a place to discuss a possible concept of
culture. A culture, from the viewpoint of this taxonomy,

is a coherent, agreed upon set of decisions as to which phenomena, entities and processes shall be considered as belonging to (being a part of, included in) which Realm. For example, shall the human body be considered as being a phenomenon of, and following the laws (basic limiting principles) of Realm i or Realm iii? The medical treatment implied is very different in the two Realms. Energy flowing through meridians and other channels is legitimate (and probably inexorable) in Realm iii. Energy does not exist in Realm i. Conversely, the four laws of Koch which determine the presence or absence of a pathogenic organism do not apply to Realm iii.

Western medicine views the body as in Realm i (the Quantitative/Discrete Realm). In this Realm one typically goes from the specific to the general. By and large Western medicine proceeds in this way. The theory basically is "If you cure the specific problem, the entire body will function better." We cut out the cancer, bring down the fever and so forth. Eastern medicine views the body as existing in Realm iii (the Non-quantitative/ Discrete Realm), where one typically goes from the general to the specific. By and large Eastern medicine tries to heal the entire body so that the specific problem will be healed by the general function of the body. If the energy flow through the body is redirected so that it is distributed and flowing properly (as by acupuncture or qigong), then the specific problems will be healed. This is a fundamental difference in approach that is rarely understood by those in conflict over the use of Eastern or

Western techniques. Without this understanding there have been few systematic efforts to experiment with combining the two.

There is a tremendous variation in the effectiveness of a large variety of medical treatments including both Western mainline treatments and those used in other cultures. It may be useful to begin to explore whether or not the effectiveness of a treatment is affected (not determined, but affected) by the presence or absence of a joint belief of physician and patient as to whether Realm i, ii, iii, or iv includes the body and its functioning. "There are nine and sixty ways of constructing tribal lays, and-every-single-one-of-them is right," Kipling wrote.[1]

It is not only the structure of the world picture we are using that determines our behavior. It is also the assumptions we make, the axioms we include. A St. Theresa and an Adolf Hitler might be using the same Kingdom and Realm in their definitions of the universe, but the assumptions are very different and therefore so is their behavior. A Jewish, a Moslem and a Christian fundamentalist may all agree on the definition of space, time, causation and identity of their world pictures, but their different assumptions may lead them to trying to kill each other. Their differences will show in the Domains of their world picture but not in its Kingdom or Realm.

VIII.
The Realms of Consciousness and Our Frequent, Strange and Inconsistent Behavior

The reason why our sentient, percipient, and thinking
ego is met nowhere within the scientific world picture
can easily be indicated in seven words. Because it is
itself that world picture. It is identical with the whole
and cannot be contained in any part of it.
— *Ervin Schrödinger*

The world picture we use changes with perceived
changes in our needs and in the environment. A shift in
either can produce an immediate and dramatic change in
consciousness. Thus our erotic orientation can change as
our perceived needs change after orgasm. The old saying that "An erect penis has no conscience" reflects the
truth in one world picture. Conscience may well suddenly return in the presence of a limp penis and other
aspects of consciousness may change as well. "There are
no atheists in foxholes" also reflects one world picture,
one state of consciousness. There may be many atheists
in civilian life, basic training or rest camp. The needs of

the individual include biological needs, the meaning of one's existence, predictability of some classes of events, individuality, relationships, etc. As a very wide variety of studies has shown, all are essential to the human being. The absence of, or too small an amount of, some need fulfillments (such as food or water) shows its effects immediately and obviously. The absence or insufficiency of others such as existential meaning may take a longer time to show effects, but the need is just as real. The fact that human beings will often sacrifice biological needs to relationships is well known and attested.

Human Contradictions

Our own feelings and behavior while using one world picture may be far different from when we are using another. Rarely aware of how we shift from one to another, we may be surprised and sometimes appalled by what we do and feel.

All through recorded history we humans often have been confused at the contradictory nature of our behavior. St. Paul wrote, "For the good that I would, I do not do, but the evil which I would not, that I do." (Romans 7:19.) The Roman poet Ovid put it:

> I hear desire say "yes" and reason "no" and see with open eyes the better cause and know it is better, yet I pursue the worse.
>
> — *Metamorphoses*, 4–18

Indeed it often seems to us as if various opinions we have and our behaviors come from a variety of sources which appear to have little communication between them.

From time to time all of us can say with the playwright:

> I do not understand my own actions for I do not what I want, but do the very thing I hate.
>
> — *Iphigenia at Aulis*

It is not only within ourselves that so often we seem helpless to come to agreement. So often we see two individuals or groups, looking at the same situation, coming to different conclusions. "Both sides," wrote Abraham Lincoln in 1862, "believe that they are fighting on the side of God." We all are so accustomed to this phenomenon — that on both sides of a dispute intelligent and trained persons deeply and passionately believe they are in the right — we hardly remark on it. And yet it is a puzzle. Very frequently the generally given answer of "self-interest" is clearly inadequate. Very often the passionate belief holds out little or no hope for personal material gain, but leads to hardship, disaster and sometimes death.

Let us, before we discuss this further, look at another familiar but puzzling type of feeling and behavior that we read about so often in our history books.

In 1918, a group of statesmen in Europe bent over a

map of the Middle East. World War I was just over and they were in the process of carving up the defeated Ottoman Empire. With strokes of a pencil and a ruler they defined on the map a new country that had never existed before — Jordan. Once it was brought into existence in this manner it was apparently real. So real did this invention out of thin air become that in a very short time many inhabitants of the area defined on the European map were willing and often eager to fight and perhaps die for it; a slur on the flag designed for it was felt as a personal slur, often to be avenged at any price. If a piece, even a very small piece, of the area defined on the map was taken by another country, this was a matter of deep personal concern, to be undone no matter what the cost in blood.

This scenario is not unusual except perhaps in the sudden definition by map makers far away and the speed of the growth of patriotic feeling. The same things that apply to Jordan seem relevant in other historical cases. In 1861 in North America there was suddenly a new country — the Confederacy — with its own revered flag, its songs such as *Dixie* and many people ready to fight and die for it. In Realm iii, the Non-quantitative/Discrete Realm, once an entity is conceived of and defined it is real. One of the proofs in the Medieval period for the existence of God was that He was perfect, the definition of perfect includes the entity being "real," and therefore God existed. There are, and were then, better logical proofs, but this one — the argument from definition — was widely believed to be valid.

If we view this behavior with the concept that our senses provide information that tells us the truth about reality and that we act on this information, the scenario makes no sense. Why should we fight and die for a name and a definition of an area of land made by arbitrary decisions? What is such a "country" that we should feel that it has "honor" and that our very life is involved in the preservation of that honor? Why, indeed, do we feel that this is the valid and honorable way to react? Further, from this viewpoint, the viewpoint of the Realm i sensory definition of reality, (read "Kansas") such a newly created country hardly possesses reality. It is not perceptible to the senses nor does it produce predictable and consistent effects on entities that are perceptible.

From the Realm iii mythic construction of reality, (read "Oz") however, *anything that is conceived of is real,* and nothing, once conceived of, is less real than anything else. Further, a part of anything is equal to the whole of it. A flag of a country and the country itself are responded to in the same manner. Spit on the flag and you *are* spitting on the country in the same manner as a believer in voodoo magic responds when he learns that a witch doctor has made a doll of him, placed a few of his hairs on its head and then stuck pins in its stomach. His pains will be real, excruciating and can kill him.

Let us be clear on one point here. The believer in voodoo is not stupid or primitive or pre-scientific. He is simply using a mythic construction of reality in an area in which the non-believer in voodoo is using a sensory one. The situation may well be reversed if the non-believer is a part of a culture at war and the believer is not. The comparisons on page 25 show how far the non-believer's construction of reality can change under these conditions. How and where we use a particular picture of reality depends on a variety of factors. Under certain conditions a world picture is stable. Under other conditions we shift easily and fluidly from one world picture or one mix of world pictures to another, often hardly if at all noticing the transition. Whichever one we are using at the moment appears to us to be the true and valid one and all others are illusion.

Sometimes a world picture widely used by a culture or subculture is superseded by the appearance of a more elegant and satisfactory one. The possibility of getting into a war offers to many people a satisfactory solution to their needs for both individuality and relationships.[1]

> The people on Fieldstone Road in Wellesley, Massachusetts, celebrated the bombing of Pearl Harbor with an enormous party. Of course the families there were well aware that war is a terrible thing and they kept saying that to each other, but they were excited, even exalted because hate for a common enemy who is a long way away can make people feel almost ennobled. The radio did not make anything clear, except that the United States had been wantonly attacked and was going to war. "We're off!" Mark Kettel said, as though the war were a horse race or a long-awaited trip.

The first thing most of the people on Fieldstone Road did was to telephone all their relatives. Families gathered. Neighbors came in, drinks were mixed, and within a few hours the street looked as though a wedding, not a war, were being celebrated in every house.

— Sloan Wilson, *Ice Brothers*[2]

Under the impact of strong stimuli the *Weltbilds* of the individuals in a group tend to synchronize and agree. War is one such strong stimulus. There are a wide range of others, some at the other extreme.

> Under cherry trees
> There are
> No strangers.
> — Issa

The Human Need for Meaning

One of the deepest human needs (although not one generally found in psychology textbooks) is the need for meaning, for context. We need our actions to make sense somehow and to have them fit into a framework larger than the actions themselves.

Francis Bacon wrote in *Of Atheism*: "I had rather believe all the fables in the legends and the *Talmud* and the *Alcoran*, than that this universal frame is without a mind."

Every perception and every action are part of the

metaphysics we are using at the moment and make sense in terms of a world picture that includes the whole universe and how it works. The person is generally unaware of this larger context, but it is there and can be shown to be there. Nothing is perceived or done that is not harmonious with the whole perceived cosmos.

> The common-sense of each people harmonizes various laws
> without one nation following the example of another.
>
> —Vico

From the viewpoint of this approach, the great, brilliant, logical systems of such men (by and large women do not seem to do this kind of thing!) as Plato, Kant, Aquinas, and Spinoza are attempts to push one world picture to its limits and then to insist that it covers and includes all reality. There is no question as to the magnificent brilliance and integrity with which these works were done, but one might as well say that Beethoven's *Ninth* or Van Gogh's *Sunflowers* include all art.

Scientists and philosophers have, since classic Greek times at any rate, been devoted to devising a general theory that would cover everything. It will probably take us a long time to fully realize that no such theory is possible. There may well be, as I am trying to show here, a general theory of theories, but that is about all. To put together a theory that would explain why Mozart moves us so much, and why people fall in love, and why babies are so cute, and how an electric light works, and why light bends around the sun, why the moon pulls the tides, why butterflies migrate and why a locomotive moves — now *that* is an awesome task. To try to put together a theory of theories seems far less overwhelming.

In many scientific and pseudo-scientific circles today there is a good deal of talk about a paradigm shift. The idea behind this is that science, and our culture generally, are in the process of changing their model of the universe, "how-things-are-and-work," from the mechanical world picture to a new one. The trouble with this talk is that it rests on the old idea that there is just one paradigm, which includes the entire cosmos. Since quantum mechanics and relativity theory, however, this is no longer valid. We do *not* need a new model of reality in the sensory realm, for example. The old one is perfectly adequate. We did need new ones in the microcosm and in the macrocosm. We developed them. We do need a new one in the realm of consciousness. We can develop it. The model will be compatible with the others in use in science, though it will be different. We do not need a "new paradigm" to cover the cosmos. We need rather to look at each realm of experience and to see what description of reality fits the data.

IX.
The Roads to Truth

Reason has moons, but moons not hers
Lie mirror'd on her sea,
Confusing her astronomers,
But O! delighting me.
— *Ralph Hodgson*

The Different Roads to Truth

The question about the correct way to find the truth about something important is a very old one. In the Medieval period there was much disagreement over whether the truth could only be arrived at by faith and revelation, by the senses, or whether there were two valid separate truths depending on which or both of these were used. Overall it was generally agreed that faith was the primary and final road to truth, at least for many questions.

In the 17th century this belief was reversed. Instead of "Men are fallible but the Bible is not, therefore faith is the only sure road," the belief became "Scripture was written by fallible men, but the senses do not lie. Therefore they are the road to truth." Descartes wrote that the *only* way to understand anything was by observation and experiment and what came to be called "the scientific method." He believed that any field which could not be studied in this way was a field in which nothing of any importance could be learned. Thus, he said, history cannot be experimented on because events could not be repeated. To study history therefore was only useful to amuse idle men, since if you studied the Roman Empire all your life, you would still not know more about it than, in his words, "was known by Cicero's servant girl." Descartes largely grandfathered the pattern of thought called "The Enlightenment," which became the prevailing belief system of the Western world from his time to the present. This metaphysical system states that the whole universe works by the same rules, that the only valid road to truth is by cold and objective observation, logic and experiment, and that all small truths and partial understandings will someday fit into one pattern. Eventually we will find the unified field theory that covers everything. Since we believed that everything worked on the same principles, and since the world as observed by the senses worked on mechanical principles, we quickly came to believe that the entire cosmos and everything in it worked on mechanical push–pull principles.

There were countercurrents of thought. Giambattista Vico in one of the truly revolutionary books of history, the *New Science*, wrote in 1709 that history could be studied, and must be studied, by a different method than the one Descartes had described and that this other method was as valid for its field as that of Descartes for the physical world.[1] Later, others such as von Herder, Windelband, Dilthey and William James expanded Vico's work, but they did not get very far in convincing the Western world. The very simplicity of the Enlightenment view made it popular, and the awesome progress it led to in physics and chemistry made it seem like *the truth* about reality.

The Enlightenment view only really began slowly to unravel in scientific circles with the advent of quantum mechanics. Max Planck, the father of that science, showed that the microcosm operated on quite different laws than did the world as revealed by the senses. (For example, cause-and-effect is not an observable at sub-atomic levels.) Einstein then demonstrated that the world of the very large and fast also had a completely different set of laws and observables. (For example, if you are an engineer and are planning a subway system for a city, you use our familiar Euclidean geometry. If you are an astronomer and dealing with the space between the stars, you use the very different Riemanian geometry in which parallel lines *do* meet and a straight line is *not* the shortest distance between two points.) Which is the *true* geometry on which the universe works? It depends on what you are trying to do. And for those of us raised in the West in the last few centuries, that is a very difficult sentence to swallow. Almost as hard an idea to absorb is that there are different legitimate ways of organizing reality and that each of these implies a different valid method to solve problems and arrive at truth. Further, that unless the particular valid method for this organization is used, the answer is invalid.

There are different methods for reaching truth, but this does *not* mean that there are equally valid, but different answers to serious questions and that we are left to take our pick according to personal choice. The valid answer to a question is the one reached by a correct use of the method applicable to the Realm in which the question exists. We ask, "What are the observables we find when we ask this question?" This tells us the Realm it is in and thus the correct method for arriving at a valid answer — the truth. Applying this we arrive at the correct and valid answer to the question. Questions answered with the use of a method of a different Realm do not lead to a valid answer. I cannot answer questions of morality, of ethics, of oughts and shoulds with the use of the empirical, going from the particular to the general, objective logic and experimentation of Realm i. The observables I am dealing with in ethical questions are not quantitative and discrete.

Applying the Concept of Realms to the Truth in Central Park's Sheep Meadow

In Central Park, in the heart of New York City there is a large and beautiful grassy field called "The Sheep

Meadow."* How do I find out the "truth" about the lovely green area in front of me? What techniques do I use to determine it? Each Realm of Experience can answer certain types of questions and cannot answer others. I find that the question I am asking as I stand on the edge of the Sheep Meadow leads me to a certain type of observable and I automatically shift the realm of experience I am a part of, just as Psmith shifted as he went through the evening at home. If I ask questions such as "What is the relationship between the amount of rain and the rate of growth of the grass?" or "How many earthworms per cubic yard are necessary for the grass to retain a specific intensity of green?" I am asking about, and observing, discrete, quantitatively describable entities and their relationships. These are Realm i observables, and questions concerning them are answerable in Realm i. In this Realm the way to truth is through an empirical approach. It is attained by going from the particular to the general. I vary the amount of water available either experimentally or through observation of the natural course of rain, dew, etc. and observe the results. I try to hold everything else constant (time of year, average temperature, etc.) and again observe the results. I formulate a *law* about the relationship and see if I can use it to predict new observations. These laws are the "truth" about the Sheep Meadow I have been looking for. They are valid because I used the appropriate

* When I was growing up — Lo! these eighty-odd years ago — there *were* sheep and a sheepfold there.

method in this Realm.

Now I shift the type of question I ask. As I look at the green field I think of people sunning themselves there in the summer and making snowmen and throwing snowballs in the winter. I ask myself how people should behave toward each other in places like this. If I spread a blanket in the warm summer sun and turn on my radio, how loudly should I play it so I get the maximum enjoyment? How about my sun-worshipping neighbors who do not care for my kind of music? What should I do if my neighbors, in their search for a summer tan, expose more skin to the sun and public gaze than I am accustomed to? I am asking questions about discrete entities (such as the loudness of my radio), but shoulds are not quantifiable so I am asking Realm iii questions. In this Realm the way to truth is by a rational approach. I go from the general to the specific. How loud (how many decibels) I should play my radio when my nearest neighbor dislikes it is determined by my general belief as to how people should treat each other, and if I should be concerned with the relationship between my enjoyment and their discomfort. The answers to these questions are, in turn, strongly affected by my belief in the overall structure of the universe: Is there a Heaven and Hell afterwards? Are human beings innately good or not? Are we tamed animals who learn best from the whip or aspiring angels who learn best from example and love, or our own combination of answers to questions such as these? I respond to my questions about park behavior in terms of these larger issues. Logic and experimental proof have little to do with my beliefs. These are techniques of Realm i and have little or no effect in Realm iii. The example and beliefs of an important person have little effect in Realm i unless they can be logically extended to a general law. In Realm iii they can have a powerful and critical effect. ("Sister Mary Margaret believed in me and after a while I did too.")

In work with the Fortune Society (a group of ex-convicts turning themselves around) it was clear that a majority of recidivist prison convicts changed their behavior and lives due to one person who cared about them and made this plain over time. Logic played no part in these life changeovers. In Realm iii, logical proof is of no more importance to a life change than it is to the beliefs of a dedicated Marxist, psychoanalyst, or astrologer. Or, logically proving to a person in a depression that he or she has nothing to be depressed about. Or, as Jacques Maritain put it in a somewhat different context: "The rational *demonstration* so dear to the Thomist and the experimental *verification* so dear to the Pragmatist."[2]

In Realm iii the whole is a pattern and the parts only make sense in terms of it. Unless you understand or intuit everything, you understand nothing. Oughts and shoulds have their roots here. The whole determines the parts and a truth feels right in terms of the general pattern and is sought there. If it feels wrong it is not a valid truth.

Again I shift the type of question I am asking. I ask

about the total pattern of the life and matter in the Sheep Meadow. What is its overall ecology? How do all the elements, air, water, the gene patterns of grass, insects and other animals interact over time? Here I am trying to find general factors which I cannot directly observe and which make up the dynamic and structure of the field. I assemble all the specific data I can and then try to design the simplest, most elegant hypotheses I can to account for them. The truth of these hypotheses lies in their generality, and their elegance. They must have mathematical constants so that they can be tested experimentally. My hypotheses, the observables I infer, are quantitative but not discrete. A classic example we are all aware of is gravitation. The existence of a universal ether was for centuries the best and most elegant way to explain various phenomena such as the propagation of light in a vacuum. When it no longer fit the data it was abandoned. If a more elegant hypothesis that explains the data, or explains more of it, can be designed, then the first one is discarded and the new one accepted until it too is outmoded. The search for truth in Realm ii is the design of invisible variables that explain the data we have, predict new data, have mathematical constants and are the simplest and most elegant hypotheses we can make at this time.

Again I shift the type of question which I am asking. I say "What is the relation of this field to the rest of the cosmos?" "How does the entire universe work so that this field is an integral and inexorable part of it which cannot be meaningfully separated?" "Why is this field here?" "Why is the universe of which it is a part here?" In effect, "What is the ecology of the cosmos that includes me and is reflected in this field?" "How are the field and I and everything else part of the larger whole?" This is the question which is answered in states of mystical perception such as satori, Christ consciousness, cosmic consciousness and others. The clearest example most of us have of this is when we look at our own minds and find that all things flow into each other, that I cannot separate my memories from my joy or sorrow, and that there are no quantitative constants. These are Realm iv observables and so the road to truth about them is the method applicable in Realm iv.

In this Realm, the method for reaching valid understanding is a direct apprehension of the cosmos and everything in it being One with no real divisions or dividing lines in it. I and the farthest star and the nearest flower and everything that was, is and will be are one. Separations are error. This Oneness is the truth. Questions in this Realm cannot be asked but the answers to large and profound questions are often given to the satisfaction of the individual involved.

The differences in this Realm between the universe, God, Brahma and Atman are structurally unimportant.

From the viewpoint of this work it is critical (and worth repeating) that unless you solve a problem with the method relevant to the Realm in which it exists (the type of observables you are dealing with), any solution you come up with will be invalid.

From the viewpoint being developed here, "science" can be defined as an unusually obstinate attempt to apply the correct methods and techniques to the solution of problems. This runs directly counter to the Enlightenment idea that there is only one correct method for all problems (that of Realm i) and if you do not or cannot use it you are not going to get very far.

This belief has been the central belief of the field of academic psychology. Sigmund Koch, in his definitive and monumental study of the field has demonstrated that beyond question and has pointed out that it is apparently the main reason that so little progress has been made.[3] That this idea is not valid and that psychology needs to use a method relevant to the type of data it has and the observables with which it deals has been long known, but only rarely acted upon. The method relevant to psychology has been described, often in detail, by a number of people. Here lies Vico's *Fantasia*. Here is Rénan's differentiation of *La Science de la Nature* from *La Science de l'Humanité*. Here is Windelband and Dilthey's *Geisteswissenschaften* and *Näturwissenschaften*. And Gordon Allport's *ideographic* and *nomothetic* methods. The methodology for the study of human inner life and behavior has been worked out and described in detail by these men and others, but largely ignored in the social sciences. When it has been used, as by Freud in psychiatry or Robin Collingwood in history, it has proven remarkably fruitful. This method has been described by the present author elsewhere[4] and this is not the place to repeat it.

The Realms and Human Death

If a problem must be addressed in terms of what Realm it is a part of, what type of observables are found when we examine it, then what are, if any, the implications for the overwhelming and inexorable human problem of what happens to the personality when the physical body dies?

We start this exploration with the fact that we perceive our body in one Realm and our self, our consciousness, in another.

We perceive our physical body as existing in Realm i, the Quantitative/Discrete Realm. It is seen as having constants that can be mathematically treated. I weigh 198¾ pounds, I am 5 feet and 11¼ inches high, have a heart rate of 73 beats per minute, am 41 years, 5 months and 2 days old, have a specific blood pressure, and so on for hundreds of exact measurements ranging from DNA factors to lung capacity. Two pints of my blood plus two pints of my blood equal four pints of my blood, and so forth.

My specific body exists discretely from other bodies and interacts with them in all sorts of ways, from fighting to ignoring to making love, and in a host of others. My arms are connected to my torso and constantly interact with all other parts of my body, but for certain purposes I can legitimately consider them as discrete and can easily consider my fingers and toes separately. Parts of my body can be separated from the rest and go their own independent ways. Thus I can cut my fingernails, go to a barber or to a bathroom. I perceive my body in Euclidean space and Newtonian time, having its own separate identity and able to cause change in other bodies physically or by giving information.

The body exists in the definition of space of Realm i, space that is empty until filled, uniform, continuous, infinite. It exists in the clock-calendar time of this Realm and has a beginning, a period of existence and an end.

The body is seen as determined—a muscle *must* contract at the instigation of a specific nerve impulse and has no free will about it. The algorithms of the body are Markovian. If we know enough about the situation (an occurrence that happens only rarely, if ever, in our present state of knowledge) we could predict exactly and precisely what will happen next.

This is a primary perception. It is how, in Western culture at least, we perceive the physical body. With different amounts of knowledge about physiology and anatomy this view was shared by Hippocrates, Galen, Maimonides, Pasteur, Osler, Cushing and Pauling. It is, in our culture at any rate, "only common sense."

Our primary perception of the self, of me, of our own consciousness, however, is very different. We perceive our consciousness as existing in the Non-quantitative/Continuous Realm, Realm iv.

I look within and find no constants that can be mathematically treated. My feelings vary in intensity but about the best I can do to describe this variation is to describe them as less, about the same, more, and much more. I cannot say that my love for you today is 3.7 times as great as it was yesterday. Two ideas plus two ideas do not add up to four ideas. Their sum may vary unpredictably from zero to a host of new perceptions and concepts.

There are no parts of my inner being, my self, that are even as separate as are my hands and my knees. I cannot separate an idea from the feelings I have about it. Everything flows into everything else and a change in one part affects all of my inner being. It is indeed a seamless garment. Although I perceive my self to be separate from other selves and interacting with them, I find no separate parts within my self.

My self does not exist in Euclidean space. It has no precise location, spatial size, surface nor borders. No parts of it (to the degree that there are such entities) can be related spatially to any other. My anxiety about our relationship is not to the left of my childhood memories of playing on the Atlantic beaches. The geometry of the self in relationship to what is perceived as outside of itself is personal. The distance from my self to other selves or places is in terms of my feelings and of the obstacles and possibilities in the intervening spaces. I am closer to the lover to whom I am flying than I am to my seatmate on the airplane. Space is not uniform, continuous, infinite. There *is* a center to the universe from which all time and space is measured—a hitching post. It is where I perceive my self *now*. Nor does the inflexible, one-directional, absolutely uniform flow of Newtonian time exist for the self. Everything that is, was and will be, *exists*. (Freud, for example, used the metaphor that the human mind was like the city of Rome with all the buildings of ancient and modern times standing in their original positions.)

Free will is an observable that appears when we look inward at the self. It is not an observable in Realm i. Other observables such as feelings also appear that do not exist in the Realm in which we perceive the body to exist. We may anthropomorphize machines, but we are clear that the bulldozer is not angry or stubborn. (One major scientific conference came to the conclusion that the most important difference between the human mind and computers is the ability to be lovable and love!)[5]

This overall view of the inner life is a primary perception. It is how, in the Western world at least, we perceive the self, the I, our consciousness. Regardless of our theoretical conceptions of others or of humankind in general, it is how we view our own self. It is what St. Augustine, Montaigne, Freud, Pavlov, Millay, Tolstoy and Hemingway saw when they looked within.

Body and mind certainly interact strongly and continuously. Theoretically (and, generally at least, practically) one cannot affect one of the two without affecting the other. However, they are imperatively perceived as existing in different Realms of Experience: as being different in essence. The very meaning of the term existence is different in these two Realms.

In Realm i in which we perceive the physical body,

everything has a beginning, a period of existence and an end. There are no exceptions to the rule "This too shall pass away." In Realm iv in which we perceive the self, there are no things and no such rules. There are no sharp beginnings and endings, but instead a flow in which entities come more sharply into definition and then may fade into less definition. If they return to salience they may be same, stronger or weaker than they were at other times. *None is permanently lost or ended*. What was *is* and *will be*.

An observable, such as the body or the self, follows the rules, the basic limiting principles of the Realm in which it is observed to exist. Once we have determined the Realm in which we perceive an observable, we can determine its further behavior from the principles of that Realm. What then can we say about the beginning and end of an observable (such as our own self) in Realm iv in which there are no beginnings and endings? The meaning of these for the physical body and for the inner self are clearly different.

This, of course, is very far from a new idea. In all cultures which we know about, there has been intense speculation about the possibility of different fates for the body and the self at the moment the physical body ceases to function. One reason for this now becomes clear: It is the primary perception that these two exist in different Realms of Experience, and in different Realms different things happen. We attain truth by using the appropriate method for the Realm. For the question with which we are working, any other method leads to invalid answers.

X.
The New Beginning

Creator and Creature
Of your own nature.
Adam come forth.
— *Ibsen*

In any new exploration, much will be raw and unfinished. There will be much that will later be discarded as incorrect and unfruitful. This is certainly true of the present work. But it *is* the opening of a new door for the study of consciousness, a subject that in the past we have been unable to bring under scientific examination in a way that would lead to new advances. The question is, "Is the approach a fruitful one?" and not "Are all the details correct?" In the words of Warren McCullough in a somewhat similar situation, "Don't bite my finger. Look where I am pointing."

If, then Socrates, we find ourselves in many points unable to make our discourse of...the universe in every way wholly consistent and exact, you must not be surprised. Nay, we must be well content if we can provide an account not less likely than another; we must remember that I who speak, and you who are my audience, are but men and should be satisfied to ask for no more than the likely story.[1]

We see, in the examples given so far, some clues as to the potential of the taxonomic approach, even in this very early stage of development, to increase our sense, our comprehension, of the human condition.

The physicist-philosopher Henry Margenau pointed out to me that one aspect of this approach is that it helps us past the problems raised by Descartes' dualism. We no longer have to deal with the problem of finding the means by which consciousness affects the body and vice versa. We have been unable to conceive a bridge between them. Today we largely try to solve the problem by theoretically treating the *res cogitans* as an epiphenomenon of the *res extensa*. As essentially a "froth on the water," or, to use a metaphor of T. J. Huxley, as the steam whistle of a locomotive.

However, this simply leads to other problems. Typical of these is what David Chalmers and others call "the hard question." Why, they ask, don't the electrochemical brain changes go on "in the dark" without any "feel?" Once we separate mind and body we cannot seem to get them together again.

The world picture approach presented here does not deal with or consider two separate entities or universes or even universes-of-discourse. It deals with organized, coherent concepts of how-things-are-and-work and compares their usefulness in different situations. This helps us avoid a lot of so far insoluble problems.

We have, in effect, changed the venue of the Cartesian problem. As Alfred Korzybski pointed out so clearly over half a century ago, when you change the level of abstraction with which you are approaching a situation the observables change, some problems disappear and new ones appear. (To repeat Max Planck's well-known words, "When you change the way you look at things, the things you are looking at change.")

There are other implications of this approach. Many conflicts over two answers to an argument take on an entirely different appearance when we look at the differences in the world pictures of the disputants. Human beings reach logical conclusions and behave reasonably and logically in terms of the interaction between the world picture they are using and the data available to them. When two individuals or groups have the same data and reach different conclusions a causal factor of the disagreement is frequently that they are integrating the data in different world pictures. Unsolvable controversy may often be solvable when dealt in terms of the different world pictures that led to the variation. In addition once this approach takes us out of the iron grip of the question of which answer is right and which is wrong, much more flexibility for synthesis and compromise appears.

If we wish to progress in our search for correlations between what is going on in the brain and what is going on in consciousness, we will have to be able to classify both types of data. We are already able to classify our observations of the brain. This taxonomy opens the door to a classification of the observables of consciousness.

If a human being is defined as an entity who designs, lives in, and is a part of different world pictures, of different Realms of Experience, at different times (while other organisms live in one Realm of Experience only, but may change the Domain they are using within that Realm), an entirely new light is cast on the problems of how to comprehend, understand and do research on the human condition.

Some of the basic questions now become:

1. How do you classify world pictures?

2. What are the effects on behavior of different world pictures? How is the legal definition of insanity affected?

3. Under what conditions do human beings design and use and change which world pictures? What are the factors affecting the choices made? How can we best conceptualize the interactions of world pictures?

4. How do you work toward the general good (e.g., end war, protect children, protect the ecology)?

5. What are the pathological and non-pathological world pictures? What definitions of pathology are fruitful?

6. How can we combine medical treatments from Realm i (as developed in Western medicine) with medical treatments from Realm iii (as developed in Eastern medicine) so as to obtain the best results in an individual case?[2]

7. How do you design psychotherapy strategies in terms of this concept?

From a taxonomy, a classification system, of world pictures, we can expect to learn to think more clearly about the different ways we organize and live in reality and about consciousness itself. We can learn about our world constructions and their interactions. We can learn how using the wrong world picture to solve a particular problem makes finding a solution impossible. We can learn how to solve many of our most obstinate disagreements and quarrels. All this we can hope for. However, we cannot reasonably hope for exactitude or precision. Two centuries after Linnaeus' work was published, the *Encyclopedia Britannica* would correctly state: "At present, the classification of living things is a rough, non-quantitative sketch of their diversity."[3]

Life is far too rich and vibrant to fit exactly into any human-made theories or constructs ("Grey are all your theories, but green the golden tree of life," wrote Goethe[4]). Nevertheless, no one with scientific knowledge would question the tremendous value of Linnaeus' work, or the advantages it has led to in biology. We can learn, as we so often have, from theories and enrich our lives and become more at home with ourselves, each other and the world in which we live.*

Johann Gottfried von Herder, whose *Ideas for the Philosophy of Mankind*, (1789-1791), was one of the two great early developments of the concepts presented here, wrote that his work consisted "of stones for a building which only the centuries could finish."[5] It is now more than two centuries later and we are still in the early stages of construction. The building is barely begun.

> This is no place to stop halfway between ape and angel.
>
> — Disraeli

---

* Many discoveries are reserved for the ages still to be, when our memories shall have perished. The world is a poor affair if it does not contain matter for investigation for the whole world in every age. (Seneca, *Natural Questions*, [7.31.2].)

Appendix I
Where Does Consciousness Come From?

This section was written with the noted physicist and philosopher of science, Henry Margenau, Sterling Professor of Physics at Yale University.

Sooner or later in any exploration such as this the question of *what consciousness is* and where it comes from arises. In spite of long and serious work on this question, no generally acceptable or fruitful answer has been arrived at.

In trying to understand why there has been so little progress, it may help to examine the actual workings of those sciences which have made clear advances in prediction (and control where this is relevant) of the data in their fields of inquiry. In these sciences we find certain identical patterns of action. These include:

1. A certain "domain" of experience is chosen for study. This is a particular cross-section of experience, of "what is." For

example, one domain would be that of a flat, two-dimensional universe. We would call the science that studies this domain "plane geometry."

2. In each domain there are certain observables. These are entities or processes which can either be directly observed or inferred. In the domain of the flat, two-dimensional universe, these would be points, distances, angles, areas and lines.

Observables "appear" in a domain, but are not predictable from other domains in which they do not exist. Thus, in our plane geometry domain, the term "volume" simply has no meaning. We could not predict its existence. In a three-dimensional universe, however, volume appears. It is an observable and can be lawfully related to other observables in this domain. This domain is studied by solid geometry. In a universe with only two objects in it, triangularity does not apply. With three objects it appears as a new observable. In mechanics we deal with a domain of a limited number of particles and find as observables mass, position, velocity and acceleration. If the domain is of a very large number of interacting particles such as molecules, is called thermodynamics, and heat, volume, temperature, pressure and entropy appear as observables.

3. Some observables are defined in terms of others. Some, more elementary, are defined by the processes we use to perceive and to measure them, or to determine their presence or absence in a particular situation. Essentially we define distance (in Realm i, the Realm in which we do science)

by a procedure we follow with a ruler or a piece of string.

4. In the study of these observables, the important question asked by science is "What are the relationships of these observables to each other?" Science does *not* ask the metaphysical question "what" these observables are, or "how" they work. It studies rather how they vary in relation to the degree of presence of the other observables in this domain. Thus we do not ask "What is a point?" or "What is a line or an area?" We ask rather "How does area vary with variations in line and angle?" and "What are the laws defining these relationships?" In another domain, we do not ask "What is gravity?" but rather "What are the laws defining the relations of force with which masses of matter attract one another?"

To be sure, physicists do occasionally ask "What is gravity?" and they would be likely to answer "Gravity is a distortion of the metric of space." But this is hardly an ultimate answer in any ontological sense. For we would continue to ask "What is space?" Thus, in all instances, the answer to "What is…" leads to a sequence of answers, none of which will satisfy the ontologist while all when analyzed will merely present how one observable relates to others within the domain in question.

When Clerk Maxwell, surely one of the greatest intellects in the history of physics, applied the "What is…" question to matter and energy, he ended with:

We are acquainted with matter only as that which may

have energy communicated to it from other matter and which may, in its turn communicate energy to other matter.

Energy, on the other hand, we know only as that which, in all natural phenomena, is continually passing from one portion of matter to another.[1]

In the present work we are paraphrasing Clerk Maxwell's definition.

We only observe consciousness as it relates to objects outside itself. We only observe objects after they have been modified by consciousness.

Lord Kelvin defined physics as the analysis of matter and devoted his life to the task. However, nowhere in his extensive writing did he make any attempt to define matter. This is an extremely important methodological point in science. It is well illustrated by the old story about the professor who asked the student, "What is electricity?" The student paused and then said, "I forget." The professor responded with, "Oh my God! The only man in the world who knew and he has forgotten!"

5. It is accepted as axiomatic that all observables in a particular domain will relate lawfully to each other. This is a basic axiom of science, that the cosmos is orderly. Although this is a clear foundation-stone of modern science, there

are areas (such as parapsychology) in which its implications have not been clearly seen. However, in a domain such as thermodynamics, we are perfectly clear that if, at a particular time in the development of the field, we do not completely understand the relationships between volume, temperature and pressure, there still are such lawful relationships.

6. Observables, and the laws relating to them, are very different in different domains. Nevertheless, they are compatible. If they contradict each other, something is very wrong in the analysis. This again is an aspect of the basic faith of science in the orderliness of the universe. This is a far more complex matter than the rather cavalier treatment given in this work would indicate.[2]

These statements are widely accepted by the scientific community and well known by its members. They have critical importance for the question of "what" is consciousness.

If "Science is what scientists do," and we wish to make this a scientific procedure, then we must be clear about what scientists do *not* do as well. They do not ask large "what" questions. In the state of consciousness and the corresponding *Weltbild* in which science is done, this is not a legitimate type of question. A legitimate question is one that can be answered in the world picture which you are using at the time. In the world picture used by science one cannot ask "What is consciousness?" but one can ask how it varies in relation to other observables.

Consciousness appears in a domain, a cross-section of

experience, in which there are multiple human beings. Theoretically we might conceive of a solitary live entity which is conscious, but it calls for a forbidding amount of intellectual stretching. If that authority on anthropoids Köhler could say, "A solitary chimpanzee is not a chimpanzee," what would we say about a solitary human being? One can hardly picture a human being developing alone in the universe. We can understand the Robinson Crusoe situation, but the protagonist of the story was raised to adulthood in a multiple-person situation. We are taught by others how to perceive reality, even how to break down under overly stressful conditions, and even how to go beyond their teachings. Since the form and dynamic of our consciousness mirrors our perception of reality this too is taught us. An infant living alone, not even taught by the apes who raised Tarzan or the anthropomorphic wolves that raised Mowgli and Romulus and Remus, and developing into something remotely resembling a human being is very hard to imagine. (Indeed the few examples of children raised in such conditions who have been studied varied from human norms so far that Linneaus did not classify them as human, but as a separate species, "Homo ferus.")

We can, in a science ask questions about the relationships between the individual's consciousness under particular circumstances to other observables in the domain of multiple human beings. The overall culture, the individual's perceived needs, child-raising procedures, the physical environment, belief systems, etc., can serve as examples of the observables to which we could relate consciousness, but in this science we cannot ask "what" it is. In this particular world picture the question is as illegitimate as "What is the meaning of life?"

Certainly there are states of consciousness and corresponding world pictures in which "what" and "why" questions are legitimate. However, they are not legitimate in the world construction in which we "do" science and the endeavor in the present work is to proceed in a scientific manner.

ф

The fact that different logics are required in different realms of experience has been long known to philosophy. William of Ockham (he of "Ockham's Razor") pointed out in the 14th century that matters not accessible to the human sensory array (he used as one example the unity of God) could not be explored on rational grounds. The implications of this, however, have been accepted by only a very few. Many people, for example, have persisted in trying to explore the problem of personality survival of bodily death using a logic adapted primarily to matters accessible to the human sensory array: the logic of Realm i, the Quantitative/Discrete Realm.

In mathematics we know that different kinds of geometry are required to fit the data in different domains of experience. In the Medieval period the relations between the logic of faith and the logic of sensory perception was widely explored until the official position of the Church was established by Aquinas. Today every artist knows that logic is an extremely limited tool for exploring art. (Artists are far more aware of this than are most art critics.) Every child knows that sometimes the single word "because" is a perfectly logical and reasonable answer to many questions.

Where does consciousness come from? It "appears" under certain conditions as do volume, inertia, and gravity. To ask "why?" takes us beyond good science and, I suspect, good philosophy. We can, and do, study the laws of the interactions of say, gravity with such observables as mass and distance, but not where gravity, mass, and distance came from, at least not in Realms i and ii. The same is true of consciousness: like them, it appears and is there.

Appendix II
A Dialogue Concerning
World Pictures

In the year 1632 Galileo published a major work, *Dialogue Concerning the Two Chief World Systems: Ptolemaic and Copernican*. In it the central characters were two friends of his, Salviati and Sagredo, whom he had known "many years ago in the marvelous city of Venice." Galileo loved and respected these two men. He wrote in the introduction:

> I have decided to prolong their existence, so far as my poor abilities will permit, by reviving them in these pages of mine [as a]...public monument to my undying friendship.

I find it a pleasant conceit to portray their descendents, over twenty generations later, still seeking for deeper understanding of the relations of human beings and the universe.

This is an archaic philosophical form, hardly used at all in recent centuries. However, new wine in old bottles may sometimes be worth tasting, and the dialogue format may be helpful to us in our quest.

In order to try to further clarify a few of the implications of the concept of Realms of world pictures, let us imagine a dialogue in a tutorial on metaphysics between Dr. Salviati, a professor of philosophy, and Mr. Sagredo, her favorite graduate student. The student is, as students usually are in imaginary dialogues, an eager but incompletely educated straight man.

Prof.   You used the word "reality" last week. What does it mean? How does the world really work? In the real world, what are the rules, the basic limiting principles as C.D. Broad called them? Can you describe reality?

Stud.   There are some things I can say about it. Clearly everything that happens has a cause that preceded it in time. Things happen because they must happen in that specific way. Everything is determined by what happened before it. Space is empty, uniform and goes on in all directions forever. Here and there it is filled with matter. Time also goes on at exactly the same rate from whenever to forever, from everlasting to everlasting. (The student has been reading that beautiful 18th century mystic Thomas Traherne.) There are no differences in any part of space or of time. Einstein wrote, "There are no hitching posts in the universe." The basic limiting principles are the same everywhere and everywhen. Everything is determined by the same mechanical forces.

Prof.   Everything? Everything in the universe obeys the same laws?

Stud.   Of course. There are no exceptions. If I were a Medieval scholastic I would say that God is rational and consistent and that since He made everything, He made everything the same. (The student is showing off here as students do.) Ultimately the same mechanical forces determine how and when a leaf falls, a hot air balloon rises, a lark sings or a man gets up from his chair.

Prof.   And this is the real world, the truly valid description of reality?

Stud.   Clearly. Any other description is fantasy — fun and games. And without this view you would not survive biologically. It is the description my senses tell me is the real one and on which all science and technology are based.

Prof.   And it covers everything in the world?

Stud.   Yes, that is only common sense. (A rather startling remark for a graduate student in philosophy, but it is a widely shared belief, and he is young.)

Prof.   Including people?

Stud.   Yes, there can be no exceptions.

Prof.   So, am I determined? Do I have any free will?

Stud.   There are no exceptions. There cannot be or everything we know falls apart. We all live in the real world and follow its rules.

Prof.   How about you? Be honest with yourself now. Is your answer to this question mechanically determined and if it is, why should we pay any attention to it? Or is your answer the result of a free will examination of the problem?

Stud.   (After a long pause) I intellectually know that I have no free will, but everything in me shouts that I do. I believe that I have free will even though my examination of the real world tells me that there is no such thing. I know what Dr. Johnson meant when he said, "All theory is against free will. All experience is for it."

　　　Further, there are a lot of other differences between what I know to be true and what I believe about myself. I find space close to me different — somehow thicker, richer, more full than space at a distance. And time, for me, really started in my early childhood and will get a lot different, thinner, when I die. Euclidean geometry does not really seem to apply to my distances from others. I feel as if I am the center of everything and distances from me to others are strongly affected by my feelings. And the length of time to the future is determined by obstacles to be overcome and things that have to be done rather than just by the ticking of a clock. And in the past some things that happened to me years ago seem more recent and affect me more than some things that happened yesterday. And, in the real world, things are real only if they have consistent effects on other things. For me, in my feelings, anything I clearly conceive or feel and/or react to strongly is "real." (The student is clearly describing the Non-Quantitative/Discrete Realm, the mythic realm, No. iii.)

Prof. Let's look at this problem. I hear on the grapevine that you have a girlfriend.

Stud. (Surprised) Yes.

Prof. Do you love her?

Stud. Yes, we are engaged to be married.

Prof. Is your love real?

Stud.   Yes.

Prof.   If you bring her some flowers, which is more real, your love or the flowers?

Stud.   . . . . .

Prof.   So you find yourself in quite a dilemma. You have two descriptions — two pictures of how-the-world-is-and-works — and they are very different. One is a mechanically determined world with no free will that includes everything but you. Does it include your body?

Stud.   Yes, but not the real me.

Prof.   The other description is very different. It includes something that you feel is the real you. It is not mechanically determined. You believe that you have free will.

Stud.   In spite of the illogic of this, everything in me insists that I do have free will. This is my experience, and I cannot deny it.

Prof.   Of course not. And neither can any other person who is not insane. Imagine someone who says, "I have no free will. Everything I do or say is determined by mechanical forces. I am a robot." We would send him to a psychiatrist. But if a person with a Ph.D. stands up in a lecture hall and says, "All humans are mechanically determined and have no free will," we would call him a behaviorist or a psychoanalyst or a philosophical determinist and applaud his brilliant thinking and make him chairman of his department.

This last should be an interesting clue for your next assignment, which we will come to at the end of this session.

Stud.   But both views cannot be correct. Both logic and my feelings tell me that the universe is consistent. A part of each world description is that it is the only valid description of reality. How can I live with a foot in each of them? How can I resolve the tensions between them? The funny thing is that it is an obvious and important problem, but somehow I don't feel that there is a problem here. I feel almost as if I had solved it a long time ago. It should be emotionally pressing and important, but it's not.

Prof.   Perhaps your culture solved it for you long before you were aware that it even existed. Perhaps all cultures have to have a solution in order to survive. A culture must have technology which works according to the first description but cannot deny the imperative urgency of the second.

How does our, your, culture solve it?

Why don't we stop here for today? You think about this last question and bring in your thinking on Thursday.

On Thursday afternoon the student arrives with a bundle of notes and a rather exhausted air.

Stud.   I've given a lot of thought to that question of yours. And I've reread some of Ernst Cassirer, William James and Isaiah Berlin. Here are the very tentative conclusions I've arrived at so far.

First, my culture, Western culture generally, divides the world into two parts. The first covers things. This is the part of reality about which we have the technology to get consistent results or a good method for learning how to get these results. This part we perceive and react to in the first world description. This is the one in which everything that happens is absolutely determined by the past and present situation. In this world picture, space and time are everywhere and everywhen the same. Space is Euclidean, and time is Newtonian. A thing is real if it has consistent effects on other things and not real if it does not.

You can't answer ought questions in this world description, questions concerning moral or ethical problems. You can answer "how" questions and small "what" questions and "when" and "where" questions, but not "why" questions or large "what" questions such as "What is the meaning of life?" or "What happens when I die?"

Prof. You said there were two parts. What is the second?

Stud. The second part covers people's feelings and motivations, morals, ethics, the meaning of life and what happens when you die, and the way the universe behaves. For example, "Is the universe friendly?" Here are terribly important questions which I cannot answer in the first world description but cannot get rid of. The second part has a completely different set of rules and definitions from the first part. I use the second set also in areas where I have no technology and no real hope of getting any. In this world picture I am the center of the universe. Space is measured from me and is measured not in yards or light years, but in obstacles to be overcome. Time is measured from now to then in terms of situations to be dealt with and reacted to and problems to solve. When there are no more problems, time stops. There is an end to history. There are no details given in how we go about "living happily ever after." Nor are there any details on what happened before time started, before "Once upon a time." In this world description there is a hidden force that affects everything that happens. Some people and some places have more of this than others. Sometimes we call this luck or chi or mana or prana, or whatever. Whatever we call it, it is unevenly distributed and can often be affected by will, or prayer or ritual. Archbishop Temple said, "When I pray, coincidences start to happen."

(The student is giving a rather detailed description of the Non-quantitative/Discrete Realm, No. iii.)

Apparently there is a human need for both. The first for biological survival and perhaps other reasons. The second perhaps to give us reasons to survive. All cultures use both. Generally we seem to slip back and forth from one to the other and often mix them without much noticing what we are doing. In arguments we tend to assume that our opponent is using the same world picture that we are and tell him, "Don't be so illogical," without realizing that he is using a different world description than we are and from his viewpoint it is we who are being illogical.

Prof.   You have stated a dilemma which you say, correctly, that all human beings have. This is the need for and use of two different world pictures each of which claims to be the only true and valid way to describe reality. But you have not shown how your culture taught you to solve it, probably even before you were aware it existed.

Stud. I can only see a little way into the problem at this time. The first thing we are taught is to ignore the paradox. We simply learn to accept the fact that we believe in an orderly rational universe in which all things work in a mechanical manner and that there are some things that do not behave in this manner, "The heart has reasons of which reason does not know" kind of thing. And that, in this rational universe in which everything is rational, people fall in love, coo over babies, enjoy art, die for patriotic reasons, get into wars with each other, cheer for the Mets or the Jets, and do all sorts of other illogical things. Every now and then someone tries to explain these types of actions on logical, rational grounds. I think here of Skinner and Freud as examples, but their explanations are so patently silly that no one except a few devotees of the Master or other fanatics pay any attention. And then they believe them only for other people. Sort of "Men fall in love because of Oedipal displacements or early conditioning, but I fell in love because my wife is so lovable" sort of thing.

Prof. That's the explanation?
Stud. No, only part of it. After teaching us to ignore the

problem, our culture provides constant participation activities that are designed in terms of the basic limiting principles of the second world description. And, by the example of others, teaches us that these are a normal part of life and their rationale is not to be questioned. They *are*, and the reasons that they are, are not looked at or questioned. For example, time and space in this world picture are measured in terms of conflicts to win and obstacles to overcome. So we are presented with a constant series of conflicts that we can all get involved in without danger of physical damage if we lose one. Individuals and teams are set against one another with definite rules on how they can compete. Individuals identify with these teams or champions and get deeply involved with their success or failure. Champions and members making up the teams change, but the involvement goes right on. The Greeks had their regular Games and the Romans their gladiators, the Medieval period its champions, jousts and duels. The Byzantines got so involved in chariot teams (particularly popular were the Dinner Greens and the Sea Blues) that in the 8th century they once nearly destroyed the whole city after the equivalent of a World Series. (The student is showing off again.)

We also have regular pageants and group ceremonies from the Fourth of July parade on, and never notice that these activities are completely irrational from the view of the world which we all profess to be the real one. These are all mythic world description activities and our culture teaches us to "get into" this worldview and not question whether they are rational.

Prof.   So you think that the concept of two worldviews which human beings need and use explains our interest in sports?

Stud.   No, ma'am. It is a contribution to our understanding. There are certainly other factors, although I must admit that I am not sure now what they are. And there is also the theater, which is a beautiful reconstruction of the mythic view of the world. Each play has a beginning, a middle, and an end. There is a series of obstacles which the protagonist must attempt to overcome. Time exists only from the action that began the play to the resolution of the conflicts begun by that action. And if the only real world picture that humans needed was the alpha realm, the sensory world description, then the theater, movies and plays in general would be irrelevant to us.

Prof.   That is a good beginning, although I have some questions I will bring up in our next session. For now we will stop. Before we meet again start thinking about what the anthropologists have found in other cultures that is relevant to our discussion.

Three Months Later

During the preceding three months as Salviati has immersed himself full time in the problem, the role of teacher and student has subtly changed. They are now much more equals and sometimes *he* is the teacher.

Sagredo   Last week you demonstrated how human world pictures can be classified into four general classes or Realms. These are differentiated by the criteria of whether or not the observables are quantifiable and by whether or not they are discrete and that there are different valid methods-to-obtain-truth in the different Realms. And that some questions are legitimate and answerable in one Realm and may not be in another. Now what has this classification system to do with the great questions that we humans are constantly plagued with and that we cannot seem to either solve or to get rid of? Does your work have anything to do with these questions, including the problem of why we have never been able to solve them in a manner acceptable to all of us?

We might start with any of these such as "What is the meaning of life?" or "What happens when you die?" However let us first choose the question of the existence or non-existence of God. From the viewpoint of the classification system way of thinking about reality, does He, She or It exist, or not?

Salviati The question you ask is more complex than it looks. What you are asking for is a proof that would be acceptable to the entire human race. There are plenty of clear and powerful proofs either way — the "Argument from Design" for example — but none is generally accepted except by particular cultures at particular times.

As I pointed out last week, the only Realms in which we can find universally accepted answers to questions are those Realms in which we have technology. (Technology being defined as the ability to consistently predict our actions or observations. A 17th century Eskimo, an 18th century Apache, a 19th century Parisian, a modern quantum physicist, a cellist, a Buddhist monk and a Greek of the Classical period will all agree that if you want a stone to fly farther, you throw it harder, and that water can be used to put out a fire.)

In order to have technology, the Realm must include two axioms. The first is that the observables are quantitative. The second is that the algorithms are Markovian, that is, an effect invariably follows its cause and there is no free will operating. If the stone has free will and can decide how far it wants to fly, you cannot have technology.

Only in Realms i and ii are these conditions fulfilled. Only in these do we have the possibility of technology.

And therefore only in these two Realms do we have the possibility of a universally accepted proof of the existence of God. And in these two Realms, the question "Is there a God?" is illegitimate!

Whenever we have quantitative observables and Markovian algorithms, and consequently technology, we can legitimately deal with "how" questions (How rapidly does a stone fall from the Leaning Tower of Pisa?) and small "what" questions (What is this? It is a chair. What does this flash on the screen tell us? It tells us that a photon hit the screen at that point and at the moment of the flash.) We cannot legitimately deal with "why" questions or with large "what" questions.

When we try to answer questions relating to one Realm as they relate to another, we get into all sorts of intellectual messes. For example, love is non-quantitative and non-Markovian. It cannot be produced at will in the laboratory. To try to answer the question "Why do I love her?" as if it could be solved by the rational logic of Realm i (where the observables are discrete and quantitative and free will does not exist) leads us only to answers that are patently untrue or at best so superficial that only a bigot could accept them. I do not love her because of her cherry-red lips or even because she reminds me of my mother. (These are Realm i and ii answers to a Realm iii or iv problem.) I love her because I love her. That is a perfectly acceptable Realm iii or iv solution to the problem.

Le coeur a ses raisons que la raison ne connait pas (the heart has reasons which reason does not know) is a profound truth in spite of the efforts of behaviorists, psychoanalysts (and other universal mechanists who believe that everything belongs in Realm i) to deny it.

Elizabeth Barrett Browning knew more about the problem than Freud or Skinner.

> "If thou must love me,
> Let it be for Love's sweet sake only."

She did not attribute love to some special conditioning or to Oedipal displacement. She answers a question that is only legitimate in Realms iii and iv in a way legitimate in these Realms.

Sagredo   You seem to be saying that the question of the existence of God cannot be answered in any way which would be universally accepted. That universal acceptance can only be found where there is technology and that any Realm of world pictures dealing with technology cannot deal with such a question.

Salviati   Yes.

Sagredo   So your classification system has nothing to do with the great questions which plague us and which determine so many of our actions and conflicts. When we try to use your fourfold classification system we find that it is, as they say in Spain, "pure conversation." The mountain has labored and brought forth a mouse. Talk about a tempest in a teapot!

Salviati   No! You are missing the main part of all of this. *There is no one right way to answer all questions. There is no universal right-way-to-obtain-truth. There is a right way to answer any specific question. If you wish to answer a question, first determine what Realm of world pictures deals with that sort of question. What is the way to obtain truth in that Realm? Then you have the correct way to study, evaluate and obtain a valid answer to that particular question. The correct answer to a question is the one given by the method-to-obtain-truth of that Realm.*

We discussed earlier these four Realms of Experience in which we believe that we can fit all the world pictures of which we are now aware.

They are based on the Quantitative/Non-quantitative axis and the Continuous/Discrete axis. The answer to a question is always relevant to the Realm in which you are at that moment. In Realm i, God is invented and by the rules of this Realm does not exist. In Realm iii, God is discovered, and by the rules of this Realm God is real. "Real" not in i (and ii) where our physical bodies exist — as an observable — but in Realm iii (and iv) in which our consciousness exists — as an observable.

In the case of the question, "Does God exist?" we have a large "what" question that can only be legitimately answered in Realms iii and iv. In both of these, the method-to-obtain-truth yields an answer of yes.

Their specific answers, however, differ considerably. In Realm iii, God is a specific Being or Person. In Realm iv, God is the All, the One, Brahma.

Sagredo   Granted, for the moment anyway, that you are correct — that to find the answer to a question you must use the method-to-obtain-truth of the relevant Realm. Which of these two answers is correct?

Salviati   Here you are reverting to the old idea that the universe is something out there and that our task is to discover it. From our viewpoint you equally create and discover it. And the structure you create is due to the Realm you choose. You choose a Realm (in part at least) because of your purpose at the moment.

Do you wish specific guidance as to the actions you should take that will lead to rewards in the long run? Guidance perhaps under the guise of "What is right?" "What is wrong?" "What is moral?" "What does God want from me?" "What will get me into Heaven when I die?" etc. With this motivation for the question, choose Realm iii.

Is your motivation a wish to be a part of the All? To break the boundaries of the skin and know that you are much larger in space and time than your physical sensations would indicate, to participate as fully as possible in union and communion with the cosmos? Then choose Realm iv.

In Realm iii you live after your physical death as yourself (with or without your memories, depending on the Domain of Realm ii you are using). In Realm iv you continue to live, but as a drop of water dissolved in the ocean of existence. Both Realms lead to immortality, but of vastly different kinds. Which do you want? Choose accordingly.

Now comes the hard part to accept, intellectually and emotionally. Whichever Realm you choose, if you use the relevant method–to–ob-tain–truth you get the true and valid answer to the question

In a basic way, we are doing for philosophy what Gauss, Riemann and Lobachevsky did for geometry. Prior to their work there had been a deep article of faith among mathematicians (and everyone else) that there was just one correct answer to any geometric problem. They demon-strated that there are a number of different but equally correct answers depending on the ge-ometry which you choose, and that you choose a geometry depending on your purpose at that moment.

Notes

Chapter I

1. Rollo May, *Power and Independence*, New York: Delta, 1972, p. 166.

2. Eugène Ionesco, "Eugene Ionesco in Defense of the Absurd," *New York Times*, June 15, 1988.

3. Francis Bacon, *Idols of the Tribe*, 1620.

4. Anne Cassirer welbaum, personal communication, 1990.

5. Rudyard Kipling, *The Collected Works of Rudyard Kipling*, New York: AMS Press, 1970.

Chapter II

1. Arthur Jenness, personal communication, 1943.

2. G.T. Ladd, *Elements of Physiological Psychology*, New York: C. Scribner's Sons, 1887, p. 1.

3. Franz Brentano, *Psychology from an Empirical Standpoint*, 1874.

4. G.G. Stokes, 1869 presidential address to the British Association for the Advancement of Science.

5. William James, "Does Consciousness Exist", *Essays in Radical Empiricism,* New York: Longmans, Green & Co., 1912,

reprinted in *Sciousness*, Jonathan Bricklin, ed., Guilford, CT: Eirini Press, 2007, p. 114.

6. N. Block, "Consciousness," *A Compendium to the Philosophy of Mind* (S. Gottenalan, Ed.), Blackwell, MA, 1994.

7. Thomas Metzinger, "The Problem of Consciousness," *Conscious Experience*, Paderborn, Germany: Schöingh, 1995, p. 15: In his opening article "The Problem of Consciousness" Metzinger goes on to ask the question differently: "What exactly do we want to know?"

    Much of the material presented here on the explorations of consciousness in the late 19th and early 20th centuries came from such works as E.B. Titchener, *The Postulates of a Structural Psychology*, *Philosophical Review*, 1898, Vol. 7 and E.B. Titchener, *Lecture on the Experimental Psychology of the Thought Processes*, , New York: MacMillan, 1909, and from other books of his. Also from other psychology texts of the period, such as those of Ladd and of Stout, from Thomas H. Leahey, *A History of Psychology*, Englewood Cliffs, NJ: Prentice-Hall, 1980 and from my own experience in the 1930s and 1940s.

8. Brian Josephson and Beverly Rubik, *Frontier Perspectives*, Vol. 6, No. 1, 1992, p. 15.

9. Mary Midgley, *Science and Poetry,* New York: Routledge, 2001.

10. Max Velman, "How To Define Consciousness — And

How Not To Define Consciousness," *Journal of Consciousness Studies,* 2009, 16/5, p. 139.

11. Christian de Quincey, "Switched on Consciousness," *Journal of Consciousness Studies*, 2006, 13/4, p. 7.

12. K. Pearson, *The Grammar of Science*, New York: Meridian, 1957, p. 272.

13. Arthur Eddington, *Science and the Unseen World*, New York: MacMillan, 1937, p. 54.

14. William James, *The Principles of Psychology*, 1890, reprint New York: Dover, 1950, p. 230.

15. Arthur Bower Griffiths, *Biographies of Scientific Men*, London: R. Sutton, 1912.

16. Albert Einstein, *Out of My Later Years*, New York: The Philosophical Library, 1950.

17. J.N. Findlay, in G.N.A. Vesey, *Body and Mind*, London: Allen & Unwin, 1964, p. 352.

18. Giambattista Vico, *The New Science*, 1725.

19. von Herder in Isaiah Berlin, *Vico and Herder*, New York: Random House, 1976.

20. William James, *A Pluralistic Universe*, London: Longmans, Green, and Co., 1909.

21. Lawrence LeShan and Henry Margenau, *Einstein's Space and Van Gogh's Sky*, New York: MacMillan, 1982.

22. Ruth Benedict, *Patterns of Culture*, New York: Pelican Books, 1946, p. 2: "No man ever looks at the world with pristine eyes. He sees it edited by a definite set of customs and institutions and ways of thinking."

23. Laszlo and others, *The World Futures General Evolution Studies*, Yverdon, Switzerland: Gordon and Breach Science Publishers, 1980 to present, particularly Volume 5.

24. Ervin Lazlo, *The Interconnected Universe*, London: World Scientific Publishing Co., 1995, p. 49.

25. Hans Vaihinger, *The Philosophy of "As If,"* 1911, p. 15.

26. Lawrence Binyón, *Selected Poems of Lawrence Binyón*, New York: The MacMillan Company, 1922, p. 1.

Chapter III

1. Jacques Maritain, *The Range of Reason,* New York: Charles Scribner's Sons, 1952, p. 6.

2. *Encyclopedia Britannica*, 15th Edition, Vol. 18, 1981, p. 347d.

3.

The name Linnaeus gave to each rung of the ladder	The specific category leading from animals to humans
i. Kingdom	Animalia. (All living organisms which move around and take in food.)
ii. Phylum	Chordata. (All animals having backbones.)
iii. Class	Mammalia. (All chordata who are warm-blooded, bear live young, suckle their young.)
iv. Order	Primates. (All mammals with certain special characteristics including a brain with a posterior lobe, opposable thumbs, three kinds of teeth, etc.)
v. Family	Hominidae. (All primates with special characteristics such as planned, systematic tool making, potential for culture and symbolic communication.)

vi. Genus	Homo. (Hominidae with relatively large cranial capacity, habitually erect posture, fully opposable thumbs, etc. Includes Neanderthal and Cro-Magnum Man.)
vii. Species	Homo sapiens. (Modern human beings.)

4. Renee Haynes, *The Seeing Eye, The Seeing I*, London: Hutchinson, 1992, p. 6.

5. Henri Bergson, quoted in R. Haynes, *The Seeing Eye, The Seeing I,* London: Hutchinson, 1982, p. 63.

6. Herman Weyl, *Philosophy of Mathematics and Natural Science*, Princeton, N.J.: Princeton University Press, 1949.

The world picture of quantum physics and that of relativity theory are very different. John Horgan (*The New York Times*, 12 August 2005, p. 19) wrote: "[The two theories] employ very different mathematical languages and describe very different worlds, one lumpy and random and the other seamless and determined."

7. Lev Landau and G.B. Rumer, tr. M. Kemmet, *What Is Relativity?*, New York: Basic Books, 1960, p. 37.

8. See Lawrence LeShan, *The Medium, the Mystic and the Physicist*, New York: Viking, 1974.

9. Ruth Noble, *Ethology*, New York: Doubleday, 1993.

Chapter IV
1. Baudelaire, tr. Fowlie, *Les Fleurs du mal*, New York: Bantam Books, 1963, p. 25.

2. Christopher Isherwood, *Ramakrishna and His Disciples*, New York: Simon and Schuster, 1965, p. 123.

3. See LeShan, *The Medium, the Mystic and the Physicist*.

Chapter V
1. Bronisław Malinowski, *Argonauts of the Western Pacific*, New York: E.P. Dutton, 1922.

2. Ernst Cassirer, *The Myth of the State*, New Haven: Yale University Press; London: G. Cumberlege, Oxford University Press, 1946, p. 3 ff.

3. Lawrence LeShan, *The Psychology of War*, New York: Helios, 2003.

4. Bertrand Russell, *Unpopular Essays*, New York: Simon & Schuster, p. 104.

Chapter VI

1. Arthur Koestler, *The God That Failed*, New York: Columbia University Press, 2001, p. 23.

2. Max Wertheimer, *Productive Thinking*, New York: Harper & Row, 1959, p. 24.

3. Cassirer.

Chapter VII

1. Rudyard Kipling, "In the Neolithic Age," 1892.

Chapter VIII

1. LeShan, *The Psychology of War.*

2. Sloan Wilson, *Ice Brothers*, 1979, New York: Arbor House, p. 3.

Chapter IX

1. Isaiah Berlin, *Vico and Herder*, New York: Vintage, 1976: Vico (1709) was the first to point out that human beings structurally are not static and unalterable, but in their efforts to understand and transform the world they change themselves (p. xvi). He also pointed out that there is a vast difference between understanding human beings, their works and their consciousness and understanding the "external world" (p. xvii).

2. Jacques Maritain, *The Range of Reason*, New York: Charles Scribner's Sons, 1952.

3. Sigmund Koch, *A Study of a Science*, 6 Vol., New York: McGraw Hill, 1959-1963.

4. Lawrence LeShan, *The Dilemma of Psychology,* New York: Helios, 2002.

5. Symposium on Artificial Intelligence, Davos, 1984.

Chapter X

1. Warren McCullough, *Embodiments of Mind,* Cambridge, MA: M.I.T. Press, 1965, page xx.

2. In a small-scale, but ongoing study, good results have been obtained with people with cancer. (Lawrence LeShan, *Cancer as a Turning Point,* New York: Plume, 1994.)

3. *Encyclopedia Britannica*, 15th Edition, Vol. 18, 1981.

4. It must be plain by this point that I believe this classification concept to be a very important one for helping to solve the major problem of our time — comprehending more about what it means to be human and in the human condition. If we are going to be able to learn how to stop killing each other and poisoning our only planet, I believe this tool is essential. However I am in no way attempting to explain everything about us on the basis of one idea. (There is an old saying, "Don't try to make too much stew from one oyster.") Human life is far too rich for this. A concept is a tool, is an

instrument for seeing deeper and more clearly, but not for seeing everything and doing everything. How many kinds of telescopes and concepts do we need to achieve even our limited knowledge of astronomy. We human beings are at least as complex as the heavens.

Goethe pointed out that he could not "...attempt to string upon the meager thread of a single, all-comprehending idea so rich, many-colored, and complex a life as I have brought to perception in Faust..." (*Conversations with Eckermann*, May 6, 1787.)

In a similar vein, Freud wrote: "The reader need not fear that psychoanalysis...will be tempted to derive anything so complicated as religion from a single source." (*Totem and Taboo,* New York: Dodd, Mead and Co., p. 165.)

"...Nothing includes everything and dominates over everything. The word 'and' trails along after every sentence. Something always escapes." (William James, *The Pluralistic Universe*, University of Nebraska Press, 1996, p. 321. Original printing 1909.)

And Sara Teasdale showed that even the poet could not include all of a person in one poem:

I wrote you many and many a poem,
But none showed all you are.
It is as if I cast a net of words
To try to catch a star.

It is as if I curved my hand
And dipped sea water eagerly,

Only to see it lose the dark
Blue splendor of the sea.

No lens provides a glimpse of final truth (whatever, if anything, that phrase may mean!). Each one enables us to see a little more and to do a few new things. Each is blind to far more than it can see. This is as true of new conceptual tools such as this one as it is of glass telescopes and radio telescopes. And each one brings us to the awareness of new questions. Each solution is a door we laboriously open and find new closed doors behind. The possibilities for new growth and new adventures are endless!

Anything which in some sense is something thereby expresses its dependence on those ultimate principles whereby there are a variety of existences and of types of existence. (Alfred North Whitehead, *Science and Philosophy*, New York: Philosophical Library, 1945, p. 131.)

They said, "You have a blue guitar.
You do not play things as they are.

The man replied, "Things as they are
Are changed upon the blue guitar."

— Wallace Stevens

5. Johann Gottfried von Herder, *Ideas for the Philosophy of Mankind*, 1789-1791.

Appendix I

1. K. Pearson, *The Grammar of Science*, New York: Meridian, 1957, p. 272.

2. For a fuller discussion of this area, see H. Margenau, *The Nature of Physical Reality*, New York: McGraw-Hill, 1950.

3. Francis Bacon, *Of Atheism*, 1597.

4. Vico, *The New Science*, p. 311.

Index

Made in the USA
San Bernardino, CA
23 January 2015